The History of I Zingari

THE HISTORY OF I ZINGARI

R. L. Arrowsmith and
B. J. W. Hill

Foreword by
Lord Home of the Hirsel

Stanley Paul
London Melbourne Sydney Auckland Johannesburg

Stanley Paul & Co. Ltd

An imprint of the Hutchinson Publishing Group

17–21 Conway Street, London W1P 6JD

Hutchinson Group (Australia) Pty Ltd
30–32 Cremorne Street, Richmond South, Victoria 3121
PO Box 151, Broadway, New South Wales 2007

Hutchinson Group (NZ) Ltd
32–34 View Road, PO Box 40–086, Glenfield, Auckland 10

Hutchinson Group (SA) Pty Ltd
PO Box 337, Bergvlei, 2012, South Africa

First published 1982
Reprinted 1982

Set in Linotron Bembo
by Input Typesetting Ltd, London SW19 8DR

Printed in Great Britain by The Anchor Press Ltd
and bound by Wm Brendon & Son Ltd,
both of Tiptree, Essex

ISBN 0 09 150550 X

Contents

The publishers and joint authors
acknowledge the generous support
given to them by Hambros Bank

PHOTOGRAPHIC ACKNOWLEDGEMENTS

For permission to reproduce photographs included in this book, the publishers and authors would like to thank the *Auckland Star*, the Bridgeman Art Library, A. H. Brodhurst, Central Press Photos Ltd, Patrick Eagar, O. J. Grace, Clifford Haydn-Tovey, P. S. H. Lawrence, Brigadier R. Q. O. MacArthur Stanham, Marylebone Cricket Club and D. R. Stuart.

Foreword

Lord Home of the Hirsel

1846 is a long time ago, but the authors of the story of I Zingari have painted an authentic and lively picture of the Club, from the evening when it was founded in friendship, benevolence and vintage port until today, when the members can still boast that they play cricket for fun.

In the early days we were ambitious, for the Club used to challenge the Australians, and in these pages the reader will find many of the greatest names in English cricket, with their impressive deeds with bat and ball.

When the advent of the County Championship changed the whole pattern of cricket the role of IZ was clearly to promote cricket as it was played between villages and clubs all over the country. They are still the backbone of the game. The annual fixture list is the living witness that IZ is still active in that role.

When a match is won, victory is celebrated with due modesty, and when one is lost (to quote the authors) 'defeat is taken with quiet resignation, and consolation sought in the festivities provided. . . .' Long may that be the order of our cricketing days.

Preface

My first acknowledgement must clearly be to Hambros, without whose support this book could not possibly have appeared, and especially to Peter Hill Wood, who has been our advocate and ally in our dealings with them. I must admit that the prospect of trying to produce something worthy of their great generosity has been a frightening one, and I count myself lucky to have been able to enlist the help of such an accomplished writer as my old friend Bud Hill.

In considering his and my shares of the work, I am reminded of the story in Damon Runyon where the hospital is surprised to receive simultaneously from the same address 'one patient who is suffering from undernourishment and another patient who is unconscious from over-eating'. He was faced with the formidable task of selecting from and reducing to narrative form the inexhaustible riches of the IZ albums, which cover 1845 to 1914, and which, as far as I know, have never been thoroughly explored, at least with any view to publication. I, dealing with 1919 to 1981, found that for the first thirty-five years of the period no scores of minute books survive. Some scores could be recovered from newspapers and many, between 1921 and 1939, from the *Cricketer*; apart from these I had only the summary of matches given annually (with the exception of one year) in Wisden, and these are not always complete or accurate. Luckily the secretary had some miscellaneous papers, including a number of letters from the Governor 1st Wicket Down. These were helpful, but in the main I had to rely on whatever I could find in various publications and on the recollections of friends.

I have myself, too, been in fairly close touch with IZ cricket for nearly fifty years and could supply something from my own knowledge. However, I feel that I had considerably the easier part of the bargain, I could at least write without leaving my own house. I owe

Bud an enormous debt for what he has done, the more so since for much of the time his health was causing him considerable trouble and a lesser man would have abandoned the undertaking altogether.

My other debts are to the Governor for his foreword and for so kindly signing copies of the de luxe edition; to Roger Miller, who first persuaded me that this book was a practical proposition; to John Eldershaw for his admirable account of IZ Australia; to Antony Winlaw, John Tanner and Peter Stoddart for help over matches about which they know far more than I did; to Richard Long for the story of his grandfather's part in the foundation and naming of the club, a fascinating addition to our history; to our Liberal Legal Adviser, Rupert Daniels, for his advice on legal problems and for reading the text to ensure that it contains nothing actionable; to our publisher, Roddy Bloomfield, for his helpful guidance at all stages in the production of the book; and to Stephen Green, the Curator at Lord's for his assistance over illustrations. His kindness and courtesy, together with his readiness to put his considerable knowledge unreservedly at our service, have made it a pleasure to deal with him.

One notable debt I have left to the last. Our Secretary, as our members well know, lives for the Club and has thrown himself with the greatest enthusiasm into the project. He has taken from me the entire burden of the financial arrangements with both our sponsors and our publisher, with which I was wholly incompetent to deal; he has been almost solely responsible for the splendid collection of contemporary illustrations; he compiled for me the list of members; and, besides all this, he has never been too busy to answer my numerous letters by return, making many most helpful suggestions. With typical modesty and unselfishness he has always left the final decision to me and he is therefore in no way to blame for anything that is amiss. For that the responsibility is mine and mine alone.

R. L. ARROWSMITH
Amberley, June 1982

I

The Founding of the Club

WHAT better breeding ground exists for grandiose schemes and genial suggestions than the time spent after a pleasant dinner following a cricket match? In this fertile soil the seed of I Zingari was planted, and it grew and flourished mightily in an incredibly short space of time. On 4 July 1845 William Bolland took a team of friends to a cricket match at Harrow where they beat the school team with some ease. They had been driven over to Harrow by John Loraine Baldwin, who later became a co-founder of the Four-in-Hand Club and who was therefore a key figure in the transporting of IZ teams. On their return to London after the match at Harrow Baldwin invited three of the cricketers, Frederic and Spencer Ponsonby and R. P. Long, to dine at the Blenheim Hotel in Bond Street. In a discussion after supper they all agreed that the match at Harrow had been exceptionally enjoyable, not least because both teams had consisted solely of amateurs. A suggestion was made that a club should be formed exclusively for amateur cricketers who should undertake all the tasks of a cricket team without 'given men' to bolster up the bowling. It was customary for these professionals to be groundsmen at the numerous country houses whose owners included a cricket match for the entertainment of their guests. Baldwin and his fellow diners proposed to form a club that should have no ground of its own, but whose members should seek to promote the popularity of cricket far and wide. The tradition is that R. P. Long was exceptionally fond of claret and port and spent the latter part of the evening in a comatose state, but when the discussion reached the stage of a name for this their first wandering club, he suddenly murmured 'The *Zingari*, of course,' and immediately resumed his vinous slumber.

His wakeful companions eagerly accepted this title of 'the gypsies' and started framing a set of rules which were half serious, half comic and of which many have survived to the present day. They reflect the mid-nineteenth-century sense of humour, which in places is singularly childish, but at times reveals genuine wit. The opening gambit is worth remembering for its terse brevity: 'At a Meeting held . . . no matter when, and much less where . . . NOBODY, *Chairman.*'

Similarly rule 6 is eminently sensible and neatly phrased: 'That the Entrance be nothing and the Annual Subscription do not exceed the Entrance, but that the expenses of a match (i.e. of the Zingaric umpire, etc.) be defrayed by the Members engaged therein.' Rule 7 is lamentably facetious and totally irrelevant: 'That all directions connected with the game *may* be conveyed in the French or Italian languages.' However, the legislators that evening were in a playfully bibulous mood, and it would be churlish to take them to task for their occasional absurdities.

On the following day the founders informed twenty-one of their friends that they had been elected members, that William Bolland was Perpetual President and that J. L. Baldwin was Annual Vice-President, positions which both hold to this day. Despite the fact that neither of these two gentlemen were outstanding cricketers, they were admirably suited to the offices they held. Bolland was a barrister with an extensive practice and he was certainly an awesome figure of a man, six foot three in height and weighing sixteen stone. His weight increased rapidly to twenty-six stone and compelled him to retire from the cricket field, a great loss since he hit the ball with the strength of a kicking horse. He was a perfect chairman, for 'his fund of amusement, anecdote and songs kept all alive and he was never known to say an unkind thing of any person'. He might be compared without prejudice to Charles Cobham, Governor, third wicket down, whose massive frame enabled him to drive straight with such power that many an umpire flung himself to the ground as the bowler delivered the ball. As for amusement, Charles will always be remembered for his supreme skill as a *raconteur*.

Bolland died at the early age of forty-seven and was succeeded by Mr J. L. Baldwin, now called Annual Vice-President in Perpetuity, who lived to see the club complete fifty years before his death in 1896. He was not a talented player, but he had the welfare of the club at heart and did much to uphold the reputation of IZ besides organizing many items which added to the enjoyment of members both on and off the field. He kept a scrapbook, beautifully illustrated, which provides scores of matches played in the first fifty years; its twelve volumes are housed in the library at Lord's and provide fascinating material for the cricket historian and students of the social scene in the second half of the nineteenth century. There is at Lord's a handsome painting depicting Baldwin in a Bath chair with the two other surviving founders of IZ, the brothers Ponsonby, standing behind. Baldwin in profile looks vaguely disapproving while the Ponsonbys gaze fondly at their Annual Vice-President. This painting used to occupy the central position over one of the fireplaces in the old members' dining room, and on a crowded day – perhaps the Eton and Harrow match – it was a regular ploy of members and their friends to pass the long wait to get served by counting the articles in Baldwin's attire which bear the colours of IZ. Sad to relate, since the members' dining room was pulled down in 1967, the picture has been moved to the staircase leading down to the lavatories at the lower end of the pavilion. However, it is a peaceful resting place which facilitates the counting of the IZ colours in Baldwin's costume, and the highest number at present recorded would seem to be seven when wearing a topcoat and eleven in summer array. Then late in life he presided over the IZ tent at Canterbury Cricket Week as a genial autocrat festooned with emblems of the club colours and accompanied by his dachshund likewise adorned with an IZ rosette.

There is a deep and unfathomable mystery about the origin of the club colours, and it seems likely that the truth will never be discovered. In 1845 a dinner was held for which C. G. Taylor, the best amateur batsman of the period, presented colours to the club, white with a narrow pale blue stripe at intervals of about an inch. These colours, so similar to those of Cambridge, did not find favour and were replaced, possibly by R. P. Long, who was secretary of IZ at the time. A sketch dated 20 June 1846 depicts a member wearing a broad-brimmed hat whose crown is decorated with the present IZ colours arranged in segments like the Harlequin cap. Since that date the present colours appear constantly in the records. Subsequently R. P. Long related that sometime before 1845 he was travelling in Spain with two undergraduate friends from Cambridge when they met a pretty gypsy girl who, after her palm had been crossed with silver, told their fortunes. They took a fancy to a scarf she was wearing and they bought it from her. She said that the colours had a special meaning, 'Out of darkness, through fire, into light.' One of

Long's relatives came up with a slightly different version of this tale. According to this account R. P. Long recalled that he was in Spain on his honeymoon and he and his bride visited a gypsy encampment where they were greatly impressed by the performance of a dancer. The dance finished, R. P. Long asked permission to cross her palm with silver in the customary style. The girl agreed, but stated that the custom of her tribe was never to accept gifts without giving something in return. All she had was her headscarf and this she presented to Mr Long explaining that the colours of black, red and gold symbolized the history of her tribe, *I Zingari* (the Wanderers) who had escaped from slavery (black) through blood (red) to a land of promise (gold). Mr Long did not marry until 1853 and therefore this incident, if it did occur, cannot refer to the origin of IZ colours, but probably gained credence as a tradition in his family.

There is, however, a third version, contained in a speech made by Sir Spencer Ponsonby-Fane in 1904 after an IZ dinner. In it he explained that Tom Taylor, an original member of IZ, but not related to C. G. Taylor, visited Croatia seeking material for a book and brought back some handkerchiefs coloured black, red and gold; these colours were adopted by IZ as corresponding somewhat to the aims and ideals of the club. Sir Spencer at that date had been a member of IZ for fifty-eight years and his memory might have been a trifle confused. Nevertheless he had been at the very centre of the management of the club and his information may have been the most reliable. The IZ colours were, to say the least, striking, even garish, but they suited the romantic, gypsy ethos of the club. The gay colours attracted the attention of members of the MCC and in the late 1860s they produced a tie with the red and gold of IZ. This created a *furore* among the Zingari members who protested that if the MCC coloured ribbon were to be worn on a black hat, it would make the distinction between IZ and MCC membership impossible, a situation too dreadful to contemplate. However, MCC had their way, but in recent years few members have worn the red and gold tie, most of them preferring miniature MCC monograms against a dark blue background.

One final point about the colours caused a longstanding debate. Rockley Wilson's less than immaculate turnout elicited the sarcastic inquiry from a crotchety elderly member of IZ in 1936, 'Do you always wear the colours upside down?' Rockley Wilson's lightning riposte – 'Only in the year the King dies' – is alone responsible for the myth that the black band is to be worn uppermost during the period of mourning for the demise of the Sovereign.

Another episode of trifling importance has led to much argument over the years concerning the club's title, which apparently contains a grammatical error. The masculine plural in Italian of the definite article takes the form *gli* before a word beginning with a *z* instead of plain *i*. Even as late as 1935 a non-member wrote to the Governor a honeyed letter in which he made so bold as to point out that the letters in the club monogram should be 'GZ' instead of 'IZ'. The Governor must have been very restrained because his learned correspondent plunged into a flood of heartfelt thanks for taking notice of such a humble well-wisher of the club. Most members of IZ have never heard of this grammatical error, much less wanted to correct it. At a guess the fault must have originated from R. P. Long at the supper in the Blenheim Hotel in 1845. His grandson admitted that a liking for claret or port had put his relative to sleep and the founders reported that Long 'under mesmeric influence assisted at the *séance*'. It seems very probable that he was in no fit state to worry about the niceties of Italian grammar. In any case, even today the rule about *gli* is subject to regional variations, and was almost certainly not standardized in the early nineteenth century.

Yet another little-known fact about the IZ colours is that they are worn in Canterbury Cricket Week by the Old Stagers, a body which is senior to IZ by a few years. It stemmed from an amateur dramatic society formed by friends at Cambridge who were interested in acting, which started staging plays around about 1842. Most of the Old Stagers were cricketers too, and no less than thirteen of the original members of IZ, including all the officers, were Old Stagers busily engaged in performing plays during Canterbury Cricket Week to add to the gaiety of the festival. For years the Old Stagers had at their disposal on the St Lawrence ground a tent situated directly behind the famous tree in the outfield and with only a partial view of the playing area. This was not considered of any consequence since the members were too weary from acting the night before to watch the cricket *as well as* entertain the lady performers, some of whom were well-known actresses from the London stage. The Band of Brothers tent was better placed for watching the cricket; many of the Old Stagers were members of BB too and in 1973 the two tents were combined, flying the flags of BB and IZ, while the Old Stagers flag was hoisted on the military tent. With this amalgamation, permission was given for ladies to watch the cricket from the BB tent as well as use its facilities for lunch and tea. Old Stagers' performances are of a high standard and the festival ends with an epilogue composed in verse by the members, paying honour to the Spirits of Kent, IZ and BB, and continuing to entertain 'the nobility, gentry and public'.

B. J. W. HILL

2
Early IZ Matches

FOUNDING a club on 4 July does not allow much time to organize matches so late in the season, but the energy of IZ's first officers enabled two games to be arranged. The first was against Newport Pagnell on 29, 30 August 1845. It resulted in a win for the home side, but IZ, 'a new and rising club', performed creditably. Newport Pagnell batted first and scored 109, which IZ capped with a total of 113. The home side then collected 139, leaving IZ 135 to win. A gallant effort in the fourth innings ended with IZ on 96, and all parties agreed that it had been a capital game. C. G. Taylor made 55 in the first innings of IZ and was run out for 9 in the second, a calamity which probably cost IZ the match. Newport Pagnell had strengthened their team by importing four cricketers from Harrow town, but their impact on the game was relatively slight and one of the four, named Bacchus, contributed only one run to the Newport Pagnell total. The second match took place in Suffolk on 30, 31 August on a country-house ground at Campsey Ash near Woodbridge. This was much to the liking of IZ and they won in an innings, watched by a crowd of 2000 with a 'capital band which played during the whole day and with its lively polkas excited even the grave and sturdy yeoman'.

These two matches in 1845 set the club going in a spirited fashion and the President, W. P. Bolland, was able to write an optimistic review (dated 16 May 1846) of the situation now that the club was ready to face a full fixture list. The President was relieved that the club's financial position was highly satisfactory, since all the expenses of the previous year had been borne by those members of IZ who took part in the matches. He then entered a plea that, with no professionals available to help, members should make every effort to improve the bowling. The President considered this a prime essential in IZ's plans to spread the popularity of cricket throughout the country.

The first two matches in 1846 underlined the need for IZ's crusade to improve amateur bowling. Lord Stamford's XI confronted IZ with a team that contained two first-class professionals, Wisden and William Lillywhite and there was a third professional, Magniac, probably a local product, who was injured and unable to take part in the match. Even in the absence of Magniac, IZ were no match for Lord Stamford's XI, scoring 123 to their opponents' 199. The next fixture provided proof that IZ could stand up squarely to lower-grade professionals, for they inflicted a crushing defeat at Oxford on the Bullingdon team, which contained two professionals, Dean and Buttery. In reply to the Bullingdon's 128, IZ cantered home with a score of 137 for 3.

However, it was too soon to crow over a victory by an all-amateur team. In the match against Harrow School, exclusively amateur, IZ batted reasonably well to put up a total of 122 and then dismissed Harrow for 98. The bowling analyses of both sides revealed the shabby state of amateur bowling; extras amounted to 33, 24 of them being wides. The excuse for these straying deliveries was that the pitch was rough – but a wide is a wide on any sort of pitch. Another exclusively amateur match against the Eton Collegians (*sic*) saw IZ gravely humiliated; they were put out for a paltry total of 51 and the Etonians replied by scoring a lighthearted 126. All IZ could muster by way of explanation was a shambling excuse that rain had held up the start of the match.

IZ played a match against Horsham in Denne Park, a beautiful estate which its owner, C. G. Eversfield, had recently fitted up with a cricket ground. Eversfield entertained a large house party for the match. Doubtless the host had been under stress arranging all these matters, and on attempting to leave his bed on the morning after, he fell prostrate on the floor as if paralysed, 'the extremities refusing to perform their offices'. After medical treatment a doctor and a surgeon gave hopes of recovery – fortunately their optimism was not misplaced.

IZ were beginning to make a name for themselves as spirited performers and congenial opponents and were much in demand for country-house matches. The match against Hartley Row provided a close-run game which ended in a draw and the fixture attracted 'a vast concourse of spectators on both days and at one time as many as fifty carriages were on the ground, the fair occupants of which added not a little to the beauty of the scene'. Burrow Hill CC provided yet another country-house match at Dalby Hall, but it was spoiled by the fact that IZ found themselves with only seven players. The absentees subsequently claimed that letters went astray, but in the meantime the team had to be completed by local cricketers who were marked in the scorebook rather rudely as 'emergencies'. This was the first mention of these cooperative players but with the increase in the fixture list, substitutes multiplied despite the pleas from the President to 'Keep your promise. . . . Keep your temper. . . . Keep your wicket up.' The President also returned to the theme of the need to practise the science of bowling, and he must have been heartened by the successful bowling of one W. Pluckabroche (a playful pseudonym concealing the identity of W. Pickering) in the 1847 match against the Auberies, the seat of Caledon Alexander who organized a very strong club side.

1848 found IZ with a long fixture list, and difficulties arose from the Chartists' riots claiming the attention of members who had been sworn in as special constables. Nevertheless there was much cricket played and IZ had several notable successes. One particular triumph was to defeat the Bramshill CC on their ground near Strathfieldsaye. The home side had strengthened their bowling and batting by the inclusion of a couple of professionals. This formidable array of talent was put out for 47 and IZ replied with a mammoth total of 214. Bramshill fared better in their second innings, scoring 175, but this left IZ needing only 9 runs to win, which they accomplished with the loss of one wicket – a triumph alike for amateur bowling and batting. Only one criticism could be levelled against IZ: the stark phrase in the scorebook, 'The Earl of Strathmore absent without leave'.

IZ did not fare so well against a team of Present Etonians, for both their batting and bowling were mediocre in the extreme. They scored only 79 against some accurate bowling by the Etonians, who then proceeded to score 150. However, it is heartening to note that the 'annual match passed off with the greatest hilarity and pleasantness'.

In was in 1848 that IZ first took part in a match in Canterbury Cricket Week. The club had undertaken to raise a side if the advertised match should end early, and on this occasion they turned out a team to play the Gentlemen of Kent, who quickly rattled up a total of 120. N. Felix and Alfred Mynn took part in the match, but to the disappointment of the Kent supporters they scored only 1 and 3 respectively. IZ batted brightly, but time ran out when they had scored 60 for 4. However, their place in the Cricket Week was now definitely assured.

IZ suffered a heavy defeat at the Auberies, where they lost by an innings. Caledon Alexander had this time invoked the aid of Wisden among others. Faced by this talented team, IZ struggled to a mediocre total of 83, to which the Auberies replied with a score of 162. IZ then plummeted to a miserable 49 all out. The response to such defeats as this was the usual plea to strengthen the bowling, but in his letter to members for 1848 the President made no mention of the paucity of bowling talent; instead he rose to a lofty peak of rhetoric outlining how the spread of cricket was a panacea for the ills of the entire kingdom.

Hear again that happy laugh ringing from yonder group of sturdy peasants, in triumph of the downfall of the wicket of some opponent of their lord. It is not the excited laugh of revelry and dissipation issuing from the poverty-stricken frequenters of the beer-house; it is the genuine offspring of esteem and affection begotten in the service of a master who sympathizes with his lowly brethren, softens their trials, and welcomes them to a share in his pleasures and amusements. Oh! that such sympathy were more universal! If scenes such as these (many of which we have smiled upon during this cricket season) were spread more generally through our island, the monster drunkenness would disappear, with all its vicious consequences, from our villages, the beershops would be deserted, sloth would succumb to innocent and vigorous exertion, and our country gentlemen would speedily see the fruits of their good works in the healthy, honest and contented faces of the dependants on their estates in place of the sallow, cunning, bloated countenances of the session's criminals.

This is a brief quotation from a very long letter couched in heroic terms, and it is difficult to say whether Mr Bolland was sincere in his passionate praise of cricket as a social balm, or whether he was guying the lofty rhetoric of his fellow barristers. Vice-President Baldwin deemed it necessary to add to his chief's panegyric some practical advice and congratulations:

Some three years ago it was confidently asserted that we should never muster eleven gentlemen [i.e. amateurs] for any match and that unless we played players [i.e. professionals] as bowlers we never should win a match.

Most strictly have we adhered to our rule – we never have played players, much and deservedly as we appreciate them for their talents and other good qualities; the result has been different to the prognostication. Last year we played ten matches – we lost *one*. Two were undecided, but allowed by the adversaries to be very much in our favour.

B. J. W. HILL

3

IZ Spreads its Wings

In 1849 IZ began to expand its list of matches and found new fixtures mainly in the Midlands. In his letter to members dated 2 October, Mr Bolland praised Mr Baldwin for his initiative in taking on new opponents:

I have to congratulate IZ upon the increase of the number of its matches and its more than averaged success. The question in 1849 is not Where HAS the flag of IZ been unfurled? Where has it NOT? Ask the Etonian has it floated in the breeze from old silvery Thames? Has the Harrow boy watched it waving from his classic hill? Have the venerable precincts of Westminster or the more retired plains of Rugby welcomed its varied colours? Or shall we turn from lands of promise to scenes where cricket has been matured? Has Norfolk, Cambridgeshire, Kent, Hampshire, Sussex, Suffolk, Worcestershire, Essex, Berkshire, Nottingham, Warwickshire, seen us cast down or take up the proffered gauntlet? Have we kept faith with ourselves and with the public? Have we made cricket more universal? *Non mea verba*. That we have done is now an historical fact.

The Midlands provided opportunities for many enjoyable fixtures; the prosperous industrial area of the Black Country needed matches for the many new sports grounds opened by various town councils and also by the newly rich or the old families in their private parks. The first of this type of match was IZ *v*. Gentlemen of Warwickshire (with Wisden and Palethorpe) on the new ground at Leamington. IZ had a comfortable win; despite their professional assistance Warwickshire made only 57 and 34, whereas IZ countered with totals of 135 and 68. A match was played soon after against the Gentlemen of Nottingham, but IZ members were lukewarm about this fixture and four 'emergencies' had to be pressed into service.

Another new fixture was against Sevenoaks Vine, one of the oldest cricket clubs. It had been founded in 1734, and in 1773 the club was presented with the ground it still uses. A club with so long a history is likely to field strong sides, and the Vine dealt rather firmly with IZ. Batting first, IZ scored a meagre 85, to which the Vine replied with 110. In the second innings IZ fared no better than in the first, scoring 81, which left the Vine with an easy task to win; in fact, they made 162 against some moderate bowling. Perhaps this defeat was beneficial for IZ who had been having their way too easily. Certainly President Bolland, in his letter to members dated 2 October 1849, sounded slightly complacent in his long paean of praise.

His circular to members after the 1850 season was less quick to rejoice. He was blunt enough to begin with the subject of 'non-attendance' at IZ matches. 'Alas! how many unsuccessful and unfinished games would have been spared from the pages of our records but for this helot of absenteeism.' He goes on to review IZ's achievements in the first five years of the club's existence, in which IZ had 'wandered into sixteen counties'.

> We have played on 30 different cricket grounds. We have been engaged in 68 matches. We have been successful in 25, unsuccessful in 17; we had the best of 11, the worst of 8 and even in 7!! And may we not with these undoubted figures before us, exclaim with justice, 'We have done the state some service'?

The IZ fixture list grew longer and longer, and their range of matches included a game in Ireland against Phoenix Park, Dublin, which was a great success with IZ firmly on top. IZ scored 135 in the first innings, whereas Phoenix Park could achieve only 49. IZ batted again for a total of 99, which was sufficient to beat the struggling Irish eleven. Members of IZ were lavishly and hospitably entertained in the Lord Lieutenant's lodgings and attended several balls and other festivities. This was the beginning of an annual tour of Ireland which continued with a few gaps until 1906; an attempted renewal of the tour failed and this enjoyable series was the victim of the First World War in 1914.

Not to be outdone, Scotland begged for a match in 1852, and an IZ team journeyed northward to Perth on 13 September to play a local eleven on the North Inch, that huge expanse of open ground where there is space for all types of games. Perth was a dogged side unlike the mercurial Irish, and they batted almost as slowly as a modern Test match team to bring their total to 73. IZ batted with more gaiety than sense and were ousted for 62. Perth was not as successful in the second innings and crawled to 44 all out. IZ, faced with the prospect of 75 to win, were regrettably unable to reach Perth's score, being put out for 42.

1853 was a poor season for weather and all cricket was seriously affected. IZ had generously agreed to take part in a benefit match for the great Thomas Beagley, who had fallen on evil days, and in those times the beneficiary was responsible for many of the expenses of organizing a match. This arrangement continued until quite recently and the story goes that when one professional was invited to have a second benefit, he remarked, 'No thanks. I can't afford it.'

In the match on 14, 15 July when twenty-two of IZ took on William Clarke's All England XI, the weather was atrocious, but the gallant cricketers struggled undaunted amid the mud for as long as was possible and the match finished inconclusively with All England scoring 90 and 40 and IZ 102, well placed for a decisive victory. The members of IZ nobly agreed to playing a return game, this time at the Oval, and once again IZ dominated the match and won by an innings: All England were 39 and 70, while IZ made 220 for 21 wickets. It was clear that IZ could turn out a team that would match any professional eleven on equal terms, and the luckless William Clarke could in no way withstand wave over wave of high-class batting. (In fact, IZ made several appearances in first-class cricket and these are dealt with in another part of this book.) There were enough Zingaros left to carry on the role of a strong club side with distinction.

In 1858 the I Zingari song appeared, written, it was thought, by President Bolland. It has a jaunty tune that forms the solo and chorus; the words, although somewhat trite, have a jingle that would rouse the assembled cricketers late in the evening. One interesting point is that in the opening verse the poet praises the victories of the Red, White and Blue and then calls for members of I Zingari to pledge their devotion 'neath the folds of the Red, Black and Gold'. Obviously there is no attempt at making the word order conform to the meaning of the gypsy legend of the scarf.

A curious incident occurred in the IZ *v.* Royal Artillery match played at Woolwich on 13, 14 September 1858. Mr Cecil Fiennes, when attempting a delicate draw stroke, played the ball onto his pads, where it lodged until extricated by the wicketkeeper who appealed to the umpire for 'caught'. 'Out! Caught out,' replied the umpire, Mr Gollop. Only once before had such an incident been recorded (by William Ward), when a gentleman played the ball into his trouser pocket. He had immediately started to run as there were only a few runs needed to win the match, and this he certainly would have done had not a strong-armed antagonist knocked him over and, extricating the ball from his pocket, put down the wicket. R. A. Young, who played four years for Cambridge, toured Australia, played for Sussex, and was one of the few English cricketers in 1921 to score 100 against the all-conquering Australians, was involved in a similar incident. The batsman, with the ball snugly ensconced in the flap of a pad, set out for the opposing stumps, but Richard Young executed a fine rugby tackle and brought him down in the middle of the pitch. The rule for such farcical escapades was changed soon after so that any ball lodging in the batsman's clothing should be declared dead.

Another bizarre occurrence which gave cause for debate was recorded in 1873 during Canterbury Cricket Week when IZ were playing the Gentlemen of Kent.

Mr J. H. Ponsonby, in delivering a ball to Mr W. W. Rodger, obstructed it in some way with his leg, and it rolled out half way down the pitch, whereupon the batsman advanced out of his ground, hit it away and four runs were recorded, the ball at the time it was struck being perfectly still. It was the cause of some argument, some saying that it was a no-ball; the proceeding, however, was strictly in accordance with the laws of the game.

A similar occurrence took place in a house match at Eton in 1953. As the ball lay still in the middle of the pitch, the captain of the batting side shouted, 'Hit it.' The juvenile batsman, who was acutely conscious of the importance of his role, stepped forward and, taking stance, aimed a full swing at the ball. Unfortunately he lifted his head at the crucial moment and failed to hit the ball. Short leg then darted forward, seized the ball, and flung it at the stumps in a laudable effort to run the batsman out. He missed the wicket by a wide margin and the ball sped to the boundary. As with IZ, four overthrows were recorded, but an elderly house master protested that the ball had not been struck by the batsman nor had it passed the stumps and that therefore the batsman was entitled to have another shot at it, and another, and another, *ad infinitum*. Imagination boggles at the thought of a batsman instructed to play for a draw, standing over the ball in the middle of the pitch taking airshots at it until time is called.

IZ reached its zenith in the middle of the 1860s. In 1863 there was a fixture list of twenty-nine matches, mostly two-day games. It was estimated that there were about 400 members and some 100 eager to join. In the rules and regulations section, there was one of the least successful shafts of humour:

> That no Candidates be proposed unless so agreed at a meeting consisting of the P.P., A.V.P., and not less than two B.C. men. The mode of election as follows: . . . The candidate shall be placed at a wicket, with or without a bat, as the C. may decide, and be bowled at by the A.V.P. One straight ball to exclude. The number of balls given not to exceed the number of members comprising IZ.

In fact the friends or sons of the Committee were elected without much fuss, and IZ acquired a family flavour which it has never entirely lost.

The club was in high demand for matches overseas. The first request had been for a match against Phoenix Park, Dublin in 1851, and that one match burgeoned into a regular tour, although Ireland then being a part of the United Kingdom it was not considered a foreign tour. In April 1867 Paris issued an invitation for a match with the local club, all Englishmen, to be held on the Pelouse de Madrid. By special permission of the Emperor Napoleon III, the band of the Fourth Regiment of Voltigeurs de la Garde, a light infantry regiment, played a variety of delightful music. The IZ team was driven from their hotel each day to the Pelouse in four-in-hands. The players were entertained to luncheons and refreshments on the ground, and on 26 April 1867 a grand dinner was held with many toasts and speeches; the aftermath of this dinner was not shaken off by the members of the J. Zingari (*sic*) until on the following day halfway between Calais and Dover. The cricket was very briefly reported, rightly so because the match ended in a heavy defeat for the Paris club by a single innings. The reports on the match reveal an insatiable appetite for the most banal and infantile jokes in pidgin French, such as the notes for a lecture by a professional cricketer which open, 'Mossous, il fo standy uppy devang your stumps – lay stumps comprenny.' And so on.

In 1866 there were rumours that IZ were to be invited to play a match at Sandringham and at length the fixture was announced. IZ were to play against the Gentlemen of Norfolk, while IZ begged to be allowed to include HRH the Prince of Wales in their ranks. This request was granted and the Prince turned out in full IZ cricket array while 'the Princess brought sunshine each day to the field. The ground had been admirably prepared and truer wickets could not have been pitched. On both days a goodly muster of gentry and simple folk lent a varied attraction to the scene.' Norfolk batted first and scored 119, a total that satisfied the county side as an instalment, but IZ were at the top of their form. R. A. FitzGerald made 103 and Lord Skelmersdale 52 and these two were mainly responsible for the splendid score of 277. It is sad to record that HRH, batting first, was bowled for 0. After their exertions in the field Norfolk could not withstand the steady bowling of Arkwright, who took eight wickets and limited the Norfolk score to 88. Victory by an innings caused an early end to the match, but HRH, eager to 'prolong the day's amusement, instructed Major Grey to muster his Household Brigade to the number of 22 players'. A modern match manager would blench at the thought of such a command, but Major Grey performed his task admirably and every grade of employee was marshalled into service, from F. Knollys down through Francatelli, who sounds like a cook, to the humble Coggs, whose name is specially mentioned as being real, not assumed. The result was a most cheerful match with IZ easy winners over the twenty-two members of the household. HRH contributed 3 runs for IZ.

If IZ players felt weary after such an exciting two days' cricket, their spirits were raised by the gigantic meal of some eighteen dishes that greeted them that evening. Next morning they left Sandringham with the happiest memories. One final point that strikes the reader is the photograph of the two teams with IZ members looking much cleaner than usual. Mid-Victorian sportsmen liked to present a rumpled appearance, but here at Sandringham smartness was the order of the day; only FitzGerald, standing high in the back row, sported a swirling black beard and a long curling pipe.

Eton had always fielded teams that gave a good account of themselves in their IZ matches, and in 1871 reduced IZ to their lowest total ever, namely 19. Eton made 155 and then bowled their opponents out for 119. The report of this debacle was very brief and somewhat ill-mannered, merely stating, 'This match played on Saturday July 8 requires no comment. It is a curiosity in the annals of cricket and a dark page in the records of IZ.'

More prominent in the history of IZ were the huge scores made by both sides in the match against the Royal Artillery at Woolwich in 1871. IZ batted first and ran up a total of 442, the Rev. E. T. Drake being run out for 197. The Royal Artillery were defeated by an innings, scoring 214 and 164 – both respectable totals hitherto. The fact was that the science of wicket preparation had made great progress, and batsmen had eagerly seized on the opportunity for big scores. Woolwich has always been famous (sometimes infamous) for the gentleness of Artillery wickets, one of which was so easy that a fieldsman at deep square leg once borrowed a bicycle to retrieve the ball from the distant officers' mess.

At this period and for many years after, exotic titles, largely alliterative, are to be found among the Officers of IZ – Chancellor, Chaplain, Purveyor of Pantomime Properties, Xtraordinary Aide de Champ et Champs, Liberal Legal Adviser, Mutual Military Messman, Nominal Naval Navigator and Principal Post-prandial Precentor. Some of these had only a brief existence: the only one which survives today is Liberal Legal Adviser.

B. J. W. HILL

4

The Heyday of IZ

HRH the Prince of Wales continued to take an interest in IZ cricket and used to conduct parties of foreign royalty to the matches. In 1873 he and Princess Alexandra took the Tsarevitch and Tsarevna to Prince's cricket ground together with 'a brilliant assemblage of aristocratic visitors' to watch the Household Brigade play IZ in beautiful weather. It was an unfinished match, but there had been excellent play in the first two innings, with Mr Tritton batting briefly to make 64 out of a total of 187. How much the royal couple from Russia understood about the game is doubtful.

The royal visitors were lucky in one respect, namely the weather, for 1873 was one of the wettest summers ever recorded. IZ were exceptionally hardy, but even these enterprising cricketers were baulked on some occasions. One of these was a match against Mr Christy's XI on his ground at Beckenham Place Park, when not a ball was bowled. However, the splendid hospitality of Mr Christy in his lovely eighteenth-century mansion (now a municipal golf clubhouse) was a great consolation. 'The only ball called into play was that in the evening which was carried on with great spirit.' Two days later, on 16 July, IZ set out early in the train from Fenchurch Street in rain of unexampled severity to Shoeburyness, in the hope of playing against a team of the Royal Artillery which operated heavy guns made of the most colossal lumps of metal imaginable.

Sad and sodden looked Shoebury – still more sodden and sad smelt Southend – an excellent luncheon and the pleasant faces of old friends revived the drooping and dripping Wanderers at 3 p.m. A welcome break in the heavy sky held out hopes of a game, and some three hours were snatched, which was turned to advantage by the lucky batsmen. . . . 174 was totalled by six wickets. No further play took place. Saturday was employed until 1 o'clock in looking to windward and – no; we must suppress what was uttered or thought – loth to leave their hospitable friends.

A note underneath the score in the book records with some acidity, 'R. A. Fitz. . . . did not bat, W. Greenwood did not arrive, A. N. Other never came.'

Canterbury Week, however, was more fortunate. 'Lovely sunshine, toned down by a tempering wind, ushered in the early morn of Monday; and although at times the sky became overcast, the aqueous god retired before Sol's piercing rays.' Tuesday was showery and at times heavy drops fell, but 'the fair maids of Kent withstood the pluvial visitations with commendable ardour; however, although the cricketers once or twice retired from the arena altogether the day was by no means unfavourable to the noble game'. The last three days, of which two were 'Ladies' Days', enjoyed brilliant sunshine. The verbose reporter continues his learned article by noting that Terpsichore was well patronized, and that over 300 members of the county families graced the balls held on Wednesday and Friday nights. The disciples of Thespis managed to 'fret their hour' with an ability far in advance of any amateurs we ever remember. After these compliments, the reporter becomes sour, and turns his withering gaze on the cricket. All he can muster by way of praise is for the labours of the groundsman, Ladd, who had prepared some pitches in splendid condition for run-scoring (926 runs were made in the first match). A new and commodious marquee had been erected for members of the press, 'but the continuation of the cricket until 7 o'clock rendered the despatch of parcels in time for the morning papers a matter of extreme difficulty and was certainly not a practice we hope to see adhered to in the future'.

The cricket could in no wise be called remarkable except for the bowling of Mr Lipscomb, who captured the wicket of W. G. Grace for 0 in the first innings, and should have had him out for 0 in the second innings but the fielder was not ready and dropped the catch. Praise is also given to the wicketkeeping of Henty and the long-stopping of Rodger. Lord Harris also received some lofty commendation, in spite of the fact that he did not score well that year. 'His Lordship is a most excellent bat, and a rapidly improving one and it is hoped that he will find abundant opportunities for making an appearance in the cause of the county. About the rest of the batsmen both on the side of I Zingari and Kent, it is enough to observe in general terms that there was nothing of a startling nature about their

J. Loraine Baldwin,
founder and Annual Vice-President
in Perpetuity

R.P. Long
– first Secretary of IZ

C.G. Taylor

William Ward

Rt Hon. Sir Spencer Ponsonby-Fane
– one of the founders and the first Governor
(from a pencil drawing by N. Felix)

6th Earl of Dartmouth
– Governor 1st Wicket Down

7th Earl of Dartmouth
– Governor 2nd Wicket Down

Hon. Sir Edward Chandos Leigh
– for many years Secretary and later
Chancellor of IZ

W. Findlay,
for many years Secretary (left),
and Brig. W.E. Clark, for many years
Custos Rotulorum (right)

IZ v. Gentlemen of Norfolk at Sandringham, July 1866.
(*Standing*) Hon. T. de Grey, H.A. Arkwright, Hon. E. Stanhope, C.F. Buller, Lord Skelmersdale, Capt. G.H. Grey.
(*Sitting*) Lady Morton, HRH Edward Prince of Wales, Lord Suffield, W. Hart Dyke, HRH Alexandra, Princess of Wales

IZ v. Northern Nomads, 25–26 July 1900.
(*Standing*) G.F. Vernon, E.C. Mordaunt, J.A. Turner, A.G. Archer, G.J.M. Atkins.
(*Sitting*) E.G. Wynyard, H.W. Forster, F.E. Lacey, J.H.J. Hornsby, H.T. Hewitt, A.R. Don Wauchope

Lord Harris waiting to go in for Eton Rambler Second XI
on Upper Club, 4 June *c.*1919.
Leaning over him is Dr Alington, headmaster of Eton
and father-in-law of the present Governor.
The child with balloon is Giles Alington

IZ v. Winchester, 1950.
(*Back row*) T.A. Bird, Sir Derrick Bailey, Bt, R.H. Maudsley,
J.A. Darwall-Smith, J.V. Bardsley, E.F. Studd.
(*Sitting*) H.C. Pattisson, R.F.H. Darwall-Smith, R.S.G. Scott, A.E.L. Hill,
Lt R.P. Hammond-Chambers-Borgnis, RN. (*In front*) A.H. Brodhurst (umpire)

Hon. Ivo Bligh,
later 8th Earl of Darnley

A.G. Steel

G.J.V. Weigall

C. Carlos Clarke

A.C. MacLaren

Hon. F.S. Jackson

R.E. Foster

A.E.R. Gilligan

10th Viscount Cobham
– Governor 3rd Wicket Down, batting for his own
XI v. MCC touring team at Auckland, 1961.
Wicketkeeper, J.M. Parks – slip, D.R. Smith

performances.' It would have been interesting in the extreme to have been a fly on the wall at Belmont when this lofty article came to the notice of his lordship. Curiously enough, in 1875 a cricket enthusiast looking back at these matches complained that Canterbury Week had been transformed into a fashionable garden party. 'Two years ago,' he writes, 'on ladies' day there was a crowd of 14,000 two thirds of whom were looking away from the cricket.' It is not stated how these figures were arrived at, but it seems that our captious critic was right to denigrate the players.

At the end of the season of 1873 the IZ team in Ireland was touring with the greatest of pleasure, although the weather was vile beyond bearing. This time the trouble was the pitches, which were completely saturated. The cricketers of Cork were able to exploit the conditions with slow bowlers, ably supported by extremely agile fielding. IZ were all out for 35 with not a single batsman making double figures. Cork endorsed the difficulty of batting in a paddy field, but they managed to reach a total of 87. IZ struggled hard to atone for their first innings, but Cork, by more nimble fielding and especially good work by their wicketkeeper, limited the IZ batsmen to an inadequate total of 72. Cork clinched the match by scoring 21 for 3.

IZ were burning to avenge this defeat by Cork when they arrived in Dublin for their match with the Vice-Regal XIV. The groundsman had lavished every care on the wicket, but his efforts were obliterated by the torrential rain which enabled IZ to hustle out the Viceroy's batsmen for a meagre 30; once again no batsman managed to reach double figures. On a slightly less sodden pitch, IZ did well to reach 120, which seemed likely to be more than enough for their opponents; the latter, however, succeeded in scoring 124, thus setting IZ 35 runs to win, which they made for the loss of three wickets. Considering the exceptionally wet weather, the cricket had been of high quality and, as usual with the Irish tour, the entertaining was magnificent.

Another place where the hospitality was impeccable was Croxteth, near Liverpool, where Lord and Lady Sefton had their splendid country mansion. The IZ teams had of late been losing their reputation on the field of play, perhaps because the evening revels had taken pride of place. Be that as it may, on 28 July 1874 IZ set out with firm determination to restore the club's cricketing prestige. Batting first, IZ built up a reasonable score of 179 and then dismissed the Liverpool club for a mere 85 with A. J. McNeile capturing nine wickets. Unfortunately this success was not repeated in the second innings, for the IZ bowlers met with very stern resistance from the Liverpool batsmen when they followed on. The wicket had dried out and McNeile and Middleton, try as they would, could not make the ball turn. Liverpool ran up a fine score of 277; there was insufficient time for IZ to reach a winning total and they ended up with 70 for 4.

This inconclusive match was followed by a game against the Gentlemen of Lancashire, a strong and experienced side including some players who had done battle for other counties. There is a sharpish note in the report of the game indicating that a little manoeuvring had taken place, but there is no hint of actual malpractice. IZ batted first and put together a score of 159. The Lancastrians replied with a score of 130 and the match was wide open. IZ were somewhat troubled by rain, which fell heavily at one stage; even so their total of 139 was enough to give them a good chance of winning. However, in spite of good steady bowling by McNeile, the Lancastrian batsmen with a dry pitch made no mistake about winning the match with three wickets to spare. IZ bore the loss with quiet resignation and took consolation in the festive arrangements presided over by Lady Sefton.

In 1875 IZ took part in the most extraordinary match in the existence of the club. It took place on the Sappers' ground at Chatham in pleasant weather – sunny, but with a cooling breeze to keep the fielders on the alert. The Sappers won the toss and batted first on an easy paced pitch. When stumps were drawn that evening the Sappers' score was 320 without loss. Continuing next morning, the opening pair, Hon. M. G. Talbot and Mr L. K. Scott, raised the score to 356 before Talbot was run out for 172. The number three batsman, Mr. H. W. Renny-Tailyour, who had been waiting padded up for nearly a day and a half, managed to score a modest 26 before being bowled by Fryer, who was keeping a very steady length. Scott succumbed at last to Crutchley, who was also bowling well without any help from the pitch. Poor Mr. L. B. Friend, who had also waited so long padded up, lost his wicket after scoring only a single. Thereafter the IZ bowlers were subjected to a torrent of runs, although the fielders kept very much on the alert, and no chance went astray until the score was near to 500. Mr Stafford made 58, Mr Maxwell 64. Mr P. G. Von Donop reached 101 before running himself out (perhaps some military task awaited his presence). Mr Mitchell made 62 in the final stand with Mr Stratford, who was undefeated for 21 when stumps were drawn on the mammoth total of 724 for 8, which was the highest score ever recorded. The report of this match in the IZ album takes comfort from this situation by stating, 'It is always pleasant to take part in anything particularly notable and no I Zingari who assisted in this most notable match regrets his two days' outing.' The reporter continues with a hint of asperity in his remarks. 'It is scarcely necessary to speak in terms of praise of the batting of R. E. which combined the stubbornest of steadiness with the slashingest of hittiness, a combination which, favoured by good fortune, produced the hitherto unheard of total of 724 runs for eight wickets. . . . IZ ungrudingly congratulate their gallant antagonists on their brilliant performance.'

Inevitably, over the years a legend has grown up that this match involved a good deal of feeling – for instance that the Sappers were taking revenge for IZ having complained the previous year about the quality of port in the mess. So it is only right to say that there is no evidence for any of these stories. The fixture was renewed as usual next year. But perhaps the strongest evidence comes from C. W. M. Kemp, destined himself to be a Zingaro, who as a newly left Harrovian was playing for the club as an 'emergency'. His son stated that while he often talked of this match, he never mentioned any ill feeling: junior though he was, he must have known if there had been any and, if there were, he would certainly have said so. All who remember him will agree that he was one to make the best of a good story rather than to water it down.

In any event it was not until 1889 that the laws permitted a declaration, though before that sides often got out on purpose. But in this particular match it would have been farcical on the second day to have obliged ten batsmen to get themselves out with all due haste in order to enable IZ to bat, with a drawn game already the most likely outcome. So why should not the RE have some more batting practice? Only the most authoritative captains could handle the problems firmly enough to make a match out of such a situation; Lord Harris was one who could and did command his team with sufficient strength of purpose and was himself an artist at getting out deliberately without making it obvious. What did irritate IZ was the slowness of much of the Sapper batting. It is true that there were only four balls to an over in those days, and the crossing over often wasted a good deal of time. Captain Fellows claimed that he had worn a regular path in walking backwards and forwards from point to point. Also the Sappers' ground at that time was not equipped for boundaries, and every hit of any strength required a deal of running by the batsmen and by the fielders.

In this period there were many prodigious feats of run-getting and in one-day matches not infrequently only one side batted. Perhaps the most notable of huge totals was the match in 1886 between Hampstead and the Stoics (aptly named in this instance). Hampstead batted first and scored 813 in six and a quarter hours. Their last wicket fell at a few minutes before close of play, A. E. Stoddart having scored 485. Certainly a captain in those days was not eager to put his opponents in to bat after winning the toss. The RE ground continued to be the scene of prolific scores; in 1883 Lord Harris made 153 in an incredibly short time, his scoring shots including a 7, a 5 and 8 fours. On top of all this he took 12 wickets for 75. In 1935 the annual match against BB produced a combined total of 1291 runs in two days, BB scoring 403 and 256 while RE replied with 343 and 289 for 7, just 27 runs short of the winning total.

Some time after IZ's 1875 match with the Sappers, 'the "Antients" of IZ met, no matter where, with "Nobody" in the Chair, and deeply moved, passed a solemn resolution – "That the IZ bowlers who have thus distinguished themselves be, and are from this day, debarred from so distinguishing themselves again in the service of the club".'

Earlier, that season, IZ had suffered a crushing blow from their old enemy, Eton. 'Saturday June 19th IZ were beaten in one innings thanks to certain gentlemen who preferred their insides to the interests of IZ, their dinner to their duty to their club and who were found absent when called on to go in for the second innings.' Their names were 'Captain Rowley, W. Evetts, Captain Kenyon Slaney, Lord Lanesborough'. IZ scored 91 and 24 to Eton's 125. No mention is made of the weather, which was very wet in 1875, and perhaps the absentees thought that the match had been abandoned after the first innings had been completed. No doubt they had to listen to some forceful comments from the Annual Vice-President, who was particularly sensitive to any behaviour which marred the reputation of the club.

IZ fixtures continued to be beset by the need to enrol 'emergencies' from their opponents. The worst example in the annals of IZ occurred in the match against New Forest Rangers in 1876. 'Alas! on the roll being called only five Zingari responded to the call of duty: briefs, business, and loss of memory had played sad havoc in their ranks.'

Of these 'faithful five', two were found to be 'suffering from the fashionable complaint of sprained ankles'. The Rangers 'ar-Ranged themselves about the field' and not surprisingly proved much too good for their weakened visitors. An inquest on a similar defeat at the hands of the Royal Engineers (also in 1876) concludes by rising to dizzy heights of facetiousness, 'The jury returned a verdict of accidental defeat, caused by the absence of some person or persons unknown.'

1876 saw a notable IZ performance against Harrow, with the school side skittled out for 37 ('None could resist the terrific bowling of Higgins and Francis'). Against Eton, however, IZ were not so successful. A remarkable report on the match describes the school eleven displaying 'both weakness of defence and utter feebleness of hitting', but despite these sad deficiencies Eton were victorious by 57 runs. The following year, in an exciting low-scoring match at Westminster, IZ were defeated by 6 runs in spite of the schoolboys' difficulties with Lord Londesborough's 'expresses'.

In February 1877 an IZ team suddenly appeared on the cricket ground at Lucknow in India in a match against a local side who were all English, in spite of the Parsee garb and dusky complexions of some of its members. It is true that four members of the IZ team were 'emergencies', but it was remarkable that so many Zingari could be collected in so distant an outpost of Empire. The venerable Captain Hutchinson, having been elected leader, promptly lost the toss, but his courteous opponents on ascertaining the state of the wicket insisted on IZ batting first. The visitors solved the problems presented by the unfamiliar climatic conditions reasonably well by scoring 121, of which G. A. Webbe made 50 before being run out. Lucknow found the bowling of Horner and Fisher supported by nimble fielding difficult to master, and were all out for 108 shortly before stumps were to be drawn. The two Zingari night watchmen survived unscathed and both teams then prepared for the grand ball organized by the 85th Light Infantry. IZ enjoyed themselves to the full with never a thought for the morrow. No wonder their batting was somewhat listless, and although the first five batsmen gave IZ a good start, with the Hon. M. G. Talbot making 49 supported by Copland-Crawford and Fisher, the last six batsmen could only score 17, bringing the total to 165. The local Anglo-Indians also had their troubles, but their later batsmen slashed and hooked with the greatest abandon and by the close of play the score stood at 158 for 8. The match was left as a draw, a very even display by both sides and a tribute to the toughness of the Anglo-Saxons abroad.

In the home country, 1877 was a year of mixed fortunes. IZ were crushed by the School of Gunnery, whose 491 included 150 by Mr Trollope, an innings of 'good cricket and brilliant hitting' – an interesting distinction. The defeat by Hertfordshire by 11 runs would have been avoided 'had straight half volleys been a little less deadly'. On the credit side, however, there were three splendid successes. Against the Free Foresters, who were compelled to follow on, Walter Hadow's 92 not out was 'worth at least 120 at Lord's, as the long grass here stopped most of the big hits'. Against the Royal Artillery, IZ were victorious by an innings and one run, thanks in part to the home side's fielding, 'the worst that has been seen on the ground all year'. Against the Royal Engineers, P. E. Crutchley made 150 in IZ's total of 363, and against the Gentlemen of Northern Ireland, C. Marriott scored 183. On the same Irish tour IZ lost an exciting match to the Gentlemen of Ireland. The Irish were aided by an unfortunate incident in which one of their batsmen, Leland Hone, was caught and bowled by C. K. Francis. Both umpires, however, declared themselves to be unsighted and found in favour of the batsman, who then went on to make 74 not out. Despite useful scores by Colthurst, Marriott and Hadow, IZ were soon in trouble on a wet wicket against demon bowling. The *Irish Sportsman* described with picturesque hyperbole a typical four-ball over by T. Hanna: 'No. (1) A terrifically fast, well-pitched ball, generally straight. (2) A slow grub, hopping half a dozen times between the wickets. (3) A fast sneak with about two yards break on either side. (4) A slow or fast full pitch.'

In 1878 IZ took revenge on the School of Gunnery, amassing the enormous total of 573, which included centuries by P. Crutchley, H. M. Tennant and the Hon. B. Lawley. The good form was not sustained, however, and IZ were defeated by an innings by the Gentlemen of Yorkshire and were hustled out for 35 by the Gentlemen of Ireland. In the scrapbook for the year, an amusing cartoon gives one explanation for such disasters. Entitled 'The Reason Why', it shows the moonlight shining in on a table littered with packs of cards, wine glasses and empty decanters. Sometimes one wonders how IZ managed to produce any sort of cricket at all in view of the overwhelming hospitality of their hosts. A faded snapshot taken in 1893 at Culford, for example, shows a group of Zingari refreshing themselves at a table which positively sags under the weight of alcoholic stimulants.

1879 saw further reverses, with innings defeats at the hands of the Royal Military Academy, Woolwich, and the Bullingdon, while both Eton and Westminster dismissed IZ for a paltry 67 runs. The hapless School of Gunnery, however, had to endure a further onslaught from IZ batsmen, in particular C. K. Francis who made 145. Generous in victory, the report condescendingly praises Staff-Sergeant Cooke 'for his perseverance in "bowling on" so well through the long innings of the IZ'. The Royal Artillery were trounced by an innings and 58 runs, while the Gentlemen of Yorkshire were dismissed for 17 and 81 largely by the bowling of W. F. Forbes, who took 13 wickets in the match.

The following year, 1880, IZ continued on their winning way. The Royal Military Academy were dismissed for 70 in reply to IZ's score of 361. In the inaugural match of the first Lewes Cricket Week, a strong batting side proved too good for Lewes Priory, winning by an innings and 109 runs. In the match at Shorncliffe Camp, IZ came in for censure despite their innings victory. 'Delay was caused in the beginning, owing to various attractions in town overnight . . . three substitutes [were] required in place of those who had changed their minds and played elsewhere.'

These fine wins were a foretaste of IZ's performances in 1881, an *annus mirabilis* in the club's history. The season began with comfortable victories against the Royal Military Academy, Windsor Garrison, Eton, the Household Brigade and Shorncliffe Camp. IZ met their match, however, at Esher where the home side had much the better of the first innings. Only the fact that this game was played over two innings, together with lack of time, prevented Esher from forcing a win, and this enabled IZ to keep their unbeaten record. The record again survived only by the narrowest margin in the game at Rickling Green. IZ were compelled to follow on, and although they batted better in their second innings, Rickling were left with the easy task of making 63 to win. The home team were destroyed, however, by the fast bowling of C. K. Francis, and by the fact that their last man had injured himself so severely in dropping a catch at long-leg that he was unable to bat, although only 4 runs more were needed for victory. The season concluded with an innings win over the Aldershot Division. In defeating the Royal Engineers IZ made 399, their highest score of the season. The final statistics of this glorious year read, 'Played 19, Won 7, Lost 0, 12 Unfinished.'

At Oxford in 1886 IZ hammered the Bullingdon bowling for a staggering total of 658, which included centuries by four members of the side: L. K. Jarvis, Lord G. Scott, H. W. Foster and Lord Dalkeith. The game illustrates the absurd situations which could arise in the absence of a rule allowing declarations. Despite their overwhelming superiority, IZ had to bat on to the last man, and the match petered out into a tame draw. The first match involving IZ to be affected by the change in the laws that took place in 1889 is reported in 1890, when IZ were dismissed for 74 after Harrow had declared at 252 for 6.

IZ continued to put up stern opposition to stronger opponents. Against Worcestershire in August 1888 they were bowled out for 68 and made to follow on. In the second innings, after a shaky start IZ managed to reach 203, thanks in part to a ninth-wicket stand involving HRH Prince Christian, who contributed 'an exceedingly well played twenty-one' despite an injured hand. Set 84 to win, Worcestershire were soon in trouble against the bowling of P. J. de Paravincini and W. D. Llewelyn and collapsed to 65 all out. In a similar splendid recovery in the following year, IZ were 45 runs behind on the first innings in a match against the Bullingdon, but still managed to win by 2 runs in a nail-biting finish.

Not all IZ's games were so keenly contested. In the same year the match against the Athenaeum at Cambridge was abandoned by mutual consent 'owing to the counter-attraction of the polo match'. Against the First Life Guards at Windsor, cricket evidently took second place to the interest of the 'brilliant company', which included the Prince of Wales, Prince Albert Victor, the Russian Ambassador and other dignitaries. The Prince was kind enough to prolong his stay until 5.30 before leaving for a picnic at Virginia Water to the cheers of the assembled military and civilians.

In a single brilliant week in August 1890 IZ notched up a hat trick of victories against military opposition (the Royal Artillery, the Aldershot Division and the Royal Engineers), all by an innings. Country-house sides were often hard pressed to match the talents of their visitors. Hothfield Place in August 1890 fell an easy prey to the bowling of C. K. Francis and A. W. Ridley (who also made a century). After describing the feats of the IZ pair, the match report ruefully records that 'Shacklock for Hothfield Place bowled fifty overs for 119 runs and no wicket.'

If they were generous victors, IZ did not always take defeat so graciously. On the Irish tour of 1892 they easily crushed a weakened

Military of Ireland team and, perhaps overconfident after this success, were in turn defeated by an innings by a strong Gentlemen of Ireland side.

As is the custom of unsuccessful cricketers, one and all began to make excuse, and the captain was compelled to remind them, more in sorrow than in anger, that though there had been more than one doubtful decision, and one about which there was no doubt, given against them, yet

> That it wasn't the toss of the umpire,
> It wasn't the ground or the sun,
> But batting and bowling and fielding,
> Which for Ireland the victory won.

This Irish disaster is commemorated in the scrap book by a drawing of a duck pond and by this excruciating doggerel:

> The I Zingari
> Have been out on a spree,
> In Ireland no longer you'll find them.
> But leave them alone,
> They have safely got home,
> Leaving plenty of Eggs behind them.

A chronicle of IZ in the 1890s would not be complete without mention of the performance by Eton against a strong IZ eleven, including Lord Harris and the Hon. Alfred Lyttelton, in 1896. The school scored 304 for 9 declared, with 53 from B. J. T. Bosanquet (of googly fame) batting at number eight. Lord Harris was then dismissed without scoring and IZ struggled to an inglorious draw, being 87 for 7 at the close.

In 1898 the conduct of IZ on their tour of Ireland again attracted censure. In the match against the Vice-regal team, heavy rain had ensured that a draw was a near certainty. Yet, 'When a noted Zingari bat – as apart from bowler – was sent on to trundle, and when the new bowler bowled every other ball with right and left hand, it capped a climax anything but desirable. 'Tis a pity the game and desire towards definite issue was not prosecuted . . . for the sake of cricket, and more especially for the sake of the glamour that clings round the Zingari's visit, even in these days.'

B. J. W. HILL

5
The End of an Era

EVER alert to preserve the good name of IZ, J. L. Baldwin in 1889 rushed to contradict a statement in the *Field* that an IZ team had played two matches assisted by two professionals.

The IZ club was founded for the purpose of fostering amateur cricket. IZ have never employed professionals and never intend to do so. We wish it to be publicly known that the two matches in question are not admitted as I Zingari matches.

This haughty disclaimer evoked a reply from a feline correspondent who dared not reveal his identity, but signed his bitter sweet letter merely with the words, 'Good Form'. He wrote:

Sir, I notice in your paper of the 18th a letter from the committee of IZ disclaiming as IZ matches two matches reported as such in the *Field*, where professionals were engaged on their side. As these gentlemen are rightly jealous of the reputation of their distinguished club, it may interest them to know that in a match – Eastbourne *v.* I Zingari – played here on Monday last, and to which the public was charged for admission, an elderly player of the IZ team, and who was certainly old enough to have known better, was observed to be smoking a pipe while fielding during the first innings of Eastbourne. I am not prepared to state that this gentleman's efforts to stop the ball would have been more successful if he had not been smoking; but that the spectacle was an unusual one on a public ground, and set a bad example to younger cricketers.

This effusion probably had little impact on the Annual Vice-President, for the rules of the club decreed that 'the Field be under the SOLE control of the Member making the match, or of any Zingaro whom he may depute'. Nevertheless, IZ was governed autocratically, first under Bolland and after his death in 1863 by J. L. Baldwin, assisted by the Biennial Committee, of whom the leading lights were the Ponsonby brothers. The rules of the club demand complete loyalty from its members and the strictest rule was 'THAT NO MEMBER UPON ANY OCCASION PLAY AS AN OPPONENT TO IZ, EXCEPT WITH THE PERMISSION OF THE GOVERNOR IN VERY SPECIAL CIRCUMSTANCES. ANY TRANSGRESSION OF THIS RULE TO ENTAIL IMMEDIATE EXPULSION FROM THE CLUB.' This rule appears to have been transgressed on two occasions only – and immediate expulsion was the result. In July 1901 Lord Dalmeny 'having played against IZ ceased to be a member, but it having been explained that he was blameless in the matter, he was re-admitted as Agent'. The late Chief of BB, General C. W. Norman, told the story of his grandfather, who was expelled after playing for West Kent (as all his family would have done) against IZ, having previously obtained permission from the IZ captain. Not having any special influence he did not query his expulsion, but he continued to wear the club colours without anybody challenging his right to do so.

Although complete loyalty to IZ was demanded, the affairs of the club were conducted with good humour and the pages of the scrap-books are filled with genial sallies of wit and ponderous puns. The earlier albums contain many letters from members begging Bolland and, after his death, Baldwin, for permission to marry. Both the requests and the replies are couched in playful language. In 1850 Spencer Ponsonby wrote:

> Sir, in conformity with the rule of the Zingari club I beg to inform you that I am about to change my state of life, that is to leave the wandering and to take to the settled ditto. Of course I should not do this without free and full permission given under your hand and seal, and I therefore request that at your leisure you will forward to me full and free permission so to do. An answer *prepaid* will oblige, yours to command, Spencer Ponsonby.

In 1867 R. A. FitzGerald made a similar request and was sent a card decorated with IZ colours and containing the proclamation 'Know all IZ by these presents that I hereby permit R. A. FitzGerald to marry one (1) wife. J. L. Baldwin, A. V. P., IZ.' In 1871 W. M. Rose, well known for his lob bowling, presented his application for permission to marry written in verse and received the answer, 'I have great pleasure in acceding to your request on this occasion only, but beg you distinctly to understand that you must not do it again.' In

1874 Lord Harris received this brief poem wishing him and his bride the best of good fortune on their wedding day:

> Joy to ye, happy couple, is the WisH
> Echoed in each Zingaric bosom. YeA
> Right merry be your wedding morn, a faiR
> Vision of growing happiness each yeaR.
> In which bright hope, I for I ZingarI
> Send that ye wed, consent and wish succesS.

This was the work of Baldwin presumably, and although it seems inspired by the pedestrian muse, it was a kind expression of good wishes from an old friend.

As its jubilee approached, IZ had established its reputation in many parts of the world as the leading amateur club. 'The I Zingari is a sort of peripatetic MCC ready to go anywhere on cricket bent,' was the verdict of one cricketing journalist. The annual tour in Ireland was as popular with the hosts as it was with the tourists and in 1863 an Irish club was founded by Frederic Ponsonby under the name of Na Shuler. It was based on the same principles as IZ and was affiliated to it, though with its own rules and colours. When in Ireland all Zingari were honorary members and Na Shuler was very active in popularizing cricket in Ireland, despite the dampness of the weather. The First World War put an end to the club's activities and it was not resuscitated until 1935, four years before the Second World War halted its progress. A gallant effort saw it revived on a much reduced scale in 1971, by Sir William Blunden, who has kept it going ever since. In 1885 a Canadian IZ came into being, probably on the initiative of a founder member of IZ, W. P. Pickering, who lived for many years in Canada. No memory of this now survives. The Australian branch of IZ was sanctioned in 1892 and it is pleasant to record that it is still flourishing. It was founded on the recommendation of Colonel H. W. Renny-Tailyour, a notable Sapper and Kent cricketer who took part in the famous RE *v.* IZ match in 1875. A youthful Old Etonian recently back from a stay in Australia, during which he played in several of the local IZ matches, was asked for his opinion of the Australian branch; he thought for a long time before giving his verdict. 'Well, it's really the same as IZ in England – only the food is better.'

Although by 1895 IZ as a club did not furnish a team in Canterbury

Week, most of the many amateurs who took part in the County Championship matches were members of IZ and the colours were prominent everywhere on the ground. The connection with the Old Stagers was as close as ever and although fewer members of IZ actually took parts in the plays, they turned out in force for the epilogue in honour of Kent cricket combined with the spirits of IZ and BB.

With IZ's close association with Canterbury, it might have appeared desirable to hold the IZ jubilee match on the St Lawrence Ground, but Lord's was preferred as the venue for a memorial match against the Gentlemen of England. The reason for this choice is not known, but it is quite understandable that IZ should opt for the 'Cathedral of Cricket' as Sir Robert Menzies used to call Lord's, especially as a first class match there between two amateur teams was a rare and exciting spectacle which would (and did) attract a large crowd. Moreover, as can be seen from the following brief article, the arrangements for the jubilee were acceptable to the press.

This year the famous cricket club, I Zingari, celebrates its jubilee, for it was founded as long ago as 1845, in the days when there were no cricketing editions of the evening and weekly papers, no W. G. Grace, and no boundless scorers of centuries. Though the survivors of the original founders can look back across these fifty years and feel that in a measure their work is accomplished, yet the club is as active and alive as ever, and is now signalising the half-hundredth year of its existence by playing a good old fashioned match, that against the Gentlemen of England. The club from the first set itself to work to popularise cricket in the country districts, and to find out the young players who needed encouragement in the villages, while at the same time maintaining and enforcing a high standard of honour in matches, and impressing upon all young cricketers its threefold injunction – 'Keep your promise; keep your temper; keep your wicket up.' The game is now popularised all over England to an extent which even the founders of I Zingari could hardly have anticipated fifty years ago, but the club still wields its influence as an unofficial court of honour, by setting a high standard of play to cricketers of all sorts and kinds.

The author of this article had certainly been reading the letters of the Perpetual President, Mr W. P. Bolland, who emphasized the crusading role of IZ with such eloquent rhetoric. This claim to be spreading the gospel of cricket far and wide throughout the length and breadth of the kingdom is, of course, an exaggeration. Most of the would-be crusaders enjoyed playing on the many cricket grounds on private estates where their hosts entertained them in the most extravagant fashion, but it is quite true that IZ, as a wandering club, set the style for innumerable similar clubs in the middle of the last century. Indeed so many cricket clubs were celebrating their 100th anniversary in the 1950s that the MCC had difficulty in coping with the many requests for a centenary match. It might be said that IZ created an explosion of cricket in the mid-Victorian era somewhat similar to the golfing explosion of the last decade of the nineteenth century. The man who deserves the most credit for controlling this outburst of enthusiasm for cricket was without doubt Mr J. L. Baldwin, who managed the affairs of IZ so adroitly for fifty years, first as deputy to Mr Bolland and then on his own, ably assisted by the brothers Ponsonby. It was fitting that he should preside at all the celebrations of the jubilee of IZ coupled with the Old Stagers of which he was the senior member. Frail in health, he died in his eighty-seventh year on 27 November 1896.

Baldwin was a man of many parts and he was an enthusiastic club man, for besides all his work for IZ he organized the new Turf Club out of the 'disintegrated materials' of the old Arlington Club. He was an authority on card games and drew up the laws of short whist, écarté, bézique and other card games, which earned him the nickname 'King of Clubs' among his intimates. He also found time to be secretary of the Four-in-Hand Club, and it must have been a brave spectacle to witness his setting out seated on the box with the reins in his hands, skilfully directing his team of four horses, with a genial gathering of Zingaros behind him on the way to a cricket match. He was besides a notable pioneer of badminton. Finally he was a talented musician and founded a musical club. 'This Club was by some wits at once dubbed the "Pig and Whistle", and Mr Baldwin possessed among his treasures a sculptured pig with a silver whistle suspended from his neck, presented to him by a satirical lady.' Alas, no further information on this intriguing incident is available.

The obvious successor to J. L. Baldwin was Sir Spencer Ponsonby Fane, and he was duly elected at a committee meeting in July 1897 as Grand Master. It was resolved in no way to alter the constitution or rules and the election of members was to remain in the hands of the Grand Master, assisted by a unanimous committee, that is to say, one blackball to exclude as it always has and still does. In February 1898 Sir Spencer Ponsonby Fane requested that his title should be altered from Grand Master to Governor. The reason for this change is not given, but it has been suggested that he disliked being confused with a Masonic dignitary. In the foreword to the 1929 book the Governor (Lord Dartmouth) described his predecessor's rule.

Under the beneficent autocracy wielded by our first Governor, the IZ torch shone brightly. But it was an Autocracy – Innovations were sternly resisted. In those days Candidates were only proposed by Members of the Committee, some of whom presuming on their privilege, would bring forward more names than seemed necessary. It was moved to limit the number that any one member could submit. Spencer's answer was characteristic: 'I am,' he said, 'a Free-born Briton, consequently I am opposed to limiting the action of individuals.' Again when it was proposed to strengthen the rules of procedure, his answer was: 'Though approved of generally as very businesslike, it is too late in the day for IZ to be bound by *any* rules.' And so we carried on without them.

Certainly there was no lack of candidates; in May 1913 there were some eighty names put forward as candidates – seventeen were elected Members and five Agents, and in June 1914 the number of candidates had risen to ninety-five, but only eleven were elected Members and seven were appointed Agents.

The new century was ushered in in March 1900 with an unusual fixture arranged between IZ and the 'Army' during the War in South Africa. A matting wicket was set up on the veldt near Bloemfontein. The details of the scores were lost, but the approximate result is recorded as follows: IZ 51, Army 132. No doubt IZ would have given a better account of themselves had not those members who were in the Brigade of Guards been ordered to march off on the very morning of the match.

This tradition of Zingaris abroad forming themselves into sides to play the local opposition continued in the early years of the century. There are reports of two matches in India in the winter of 1904–5 (against the Calcutta Cricket Club and the United Provinces), a match in Egypt against Cairo in March 1907, and in 1914 a full-scale tour of Egypt was undertaken from which IZ returned unbeaten in their five matches, which included three 'Tests'.

The game against the Calcutta Cricket Club must rank as one of the finest in the club's history. IZ fielded a strong batting side, including such 'cracks' as Lord Hawke and A. C. MacLaren, but were soon in difficulties on an uncertain pitch and seven wickets were down for 147. At this point Lord Hawke, whom the report describes rather strangely as seeming not 'too much at home until he had made 70 or so', started to lash out in all directions and reached his century with a trio of magnificent drives, the third of which cleared the sightscreen. Lord Hawke was finally caught at the wicket for 148, 'one of the merriest knocks imaginable', and IZ closed at 346. Calcutta, with K. S. Ranjitsinjhi one of the openers, made a graceful start, but collapsed to 166 all out. General Spens elected not to enforce the follow-on, perhaps because of doubts over the stamina of his limited number of bowlers, and batted again, declaring the IZ second innings closed at 276 for 9, with large contributions from A. C. MacLaren (87) and W. M. Kington (122). This faced Calcutta with the huge task of 457 for victory, or, more realistically, of batting through the day to save a draw. That they achieved this was largely due to a superb century from Ranjitsinjhi, who began cautiously but later delighted the huge crowd, playing every variety of stroke to perfection. At the end of play Calcutta were 90 runs behind with two wickets to fall.

Lord Hawke's excellent form was not to be continued in the match against the United Provinces, where he had the misfortune to be run out before scoring. Indeed IZ's first innings only reached respectability thanks to a stand between G. Akers-Douglas (79) and General Spens (33). Lord Hawke subsequently embarked on a leisurely homeward journey via Rangoon, China, Japan and Canada, and was reported as being expected to reach England in time to captain Yorkshire in their opening match in May; such was the spacious tempo of the day.

At home the even tenor of IZ's annual round of fixtures continued with unruffled inevitability. In the scrapbooks which record their progress the facetious metaphors and dreadful puns of Victorian humorous accounts give way to more matter-of-fact match reports enlivened, however, by photographs of the participants in stilted poses. One such, in 1911, shows wicket-keeper and slip fieldsmen ruefully contemplating the outcome of a bizarre incident. 'A bowler sent up a ball which knocked one of the bails into the air. Instead of falling to the ground it lodged on the leg stump, and remained there in nice balance. The umpire decided for the batsman.' A rare touch of sophisticated humour is found in the frontispiece to the records for 1913. A sketch of a batsman, full of angular distortions, is a witty parody of the cubist trend in contemporary painting.

The club's prestige was enormous, and its principles widely respected. The Bishop of Worcester even went so far as to take the threefold rule – keep your promise, keep your temper, keep your wicket up – as the text for a New Year's letter to the diocese in 1903.

I have always thought these three very healthy and fruitful rules for life. In other words (1) to be absolutely trustworthy in regard to all undertakings, solemn and trivial; (2) to be self-controlled, and not to suffer either exasperation or disappointment to upset one's equanimity; (3) to defend the position entrusted to one, secular or religious, like a faithful soldier on guard, from all attacks, with loyalty, vigilance, and the best skill of which one is capable, and to give one's whole mind to the work with courage and hope; that is, to be a good and useful member of society.

Matches against public schools continued to provide interesting cricket. Trounced by 124 runs at Harrow in 1901, IZ returned the following year with a strong side, including F. S. Jackson. Harrow again put up stiff opposition and only a stand for the third wicket between Jackson (57) and F. Marchant (65) enabled the visitors to reach 151. Jackson was again the hero when Harrow batted; he took 5 for 33 and allowed IZ to scrape home by 17 runs. At Eton in the same year, an IZ XII were easy victors on the school's new ground at Agar's Plough. Eton must have been a popular fixture, for at the same time on Upper Club, teams from Eton and IZ were engaged in a fifteen-a-side contest.

1903 saw an overwhelming victory for IZ over the Household Brigade, who were quite outclassed by a strong side and went down by no less than an innings and 200 runs. In IZ's total of 477 for 7 declared, centuries were made by C. P. Foley and Major Greenway, while IZ's bowling was spear-headed by A. C. Macpherson, who finished with thirteen wickets in the match.

On a less exalted level than that of previous years, IZ continued to enjoy the hospitality of the owners of beautiful country houses. Generally the famous club proved too strong for their rural opponents. At Shugborough Park in August 1905, the Gentlemen of Staffordshire succumbed by ten wickets to a batting onslaught from Louis Weigall and C. D. Fisher. The following day many of the same Gentlemen reappeared under the guise of Mr W. Ward's XI, but again found the batting of Weigall, aided this time by Lord Lichfield ('despite advancing years'), too much for them.

1911 saw stirring cricket in the games against Eton and Harrow. Eton began disastrously and their first four batsmen could muster only 15 runs between them. Their later colleagues showed greater determination (in particular A. I. Steel, son of the famous A. G., who made 78), and the innings was declared closed at 323 with the last pair undefeated on 60 and 33 respectively. Steel was again a thorn in the side when IZ batted, taking five wickets, and the visitors were happy to escape with a draw very much in Eton's favour. The Harrow game was notable for the magnificent bowling of Captain Payne-Gallwey who took all ten wickets (at a cost of 75 runs). Set 158 to win, IZ lost three wickets inside the first ten minutes, and Harrow began to look like winners. They had reckoned without the redoubtable Captain Payne-Gallwey who, coming in at number nine, made top score with 44 before being bowled. Harrow finally won a thrilling match by seven runs.

In March 1914 IZ had a short tour in Egypt, their first tour outside the British Isles since 1867. They played five matches, winning three and drawing two. They beat Cairo and Alexandria and won one of their matches against All Egypt, the other two being drawn. The team was: F. H. Browning (captain), Captain the Hon. A. E. S. Mulholland, Hon. Rupert Anson, C. P. Goodden, H. C. Loyd, Hon. J. S. R. Tufton, J. R. Head, E. C. Mordaunt, Captain M. E. Crichton Maitland, Lord B. C. Gordon Lennox and H. Hesketh Prichard. Perhaps it was trustful to take only eleven. In the event, when casualties arose they were luckily able to call on two Zingaros then in Egypt, Captain F. L. Crichton Maitland and E. H. Goschen. The victory against Cairo in the first match was especially gratifying. On the first innings Cairo led by 106 and some of the local papers reported next morning that 'the visiting side contained no cricketer of value and could neither bat, bowl nor field'. However, on the second day IZ by consistent batting made 288 and bowled Cairo out for 69, Hesketh Prichard, who a few years earlier had bowled fast for the Gentlemen, taking 6 for 41. Another good game was the one-day match against Alexandria. Set only 170 to get, IZ were 13 for 3 and only a splendid innings by Tufton enabled them to win by four wickets. In the course of the tour Gordon Lennox and Anson both made centuries and invaluable all-round work was done by Mordaunt and M. E. Crichton Maitland. Of Mordaunt, for years a great stand-by both to IZ and Free Foresters, the account says, 'Throughout the tour it was only necessary for runs to be badly wanted for

Mordaunt to make them.' He also bowled very steadily. Other successes were Tufton, of whom it was said that in the slips, 'anything that was hit on either side of him within reach was out', and Loyd, who besides playing several valuable innings kept wicket superbly. 'Throughout the tour he missed very few opportunities and, in spite of occasionally appallingly inaccurate bowling, gave away scarcely any extras. One would have to look hard to find his superior among the amateur wicketkeepers of the day.' Of IZ's opponents, who were entirely English, the outstanding player seems to have been Geoffrey MacLaren, a younger brother of the great Archie. He is described as 'a batsman of the highest class, who, if he were able to play regularly, would be sure of his position as a great player'. Unfortunately his first-class career was confined to a couple of matches for Lancashire in the summer he left Harrow. Later in 1914 he was elected to IZ.

In the summer of 1914 IZ continued to fulfil their long fixture list with their usual zest, blissfully unaware that by 4 August two great nations, ruled by cousins, would be at war. Although at the request of the Government, county cricket continued till the end of August, all remaining IZ fixtures were cancelled on the outbreak of hostilities. But there were many who talked confidently of the war being over by Christmas and few could have expected that it would be five years before the club took the field again.

B. J. W. HILL

6

1915–39

On 1 December 1915, Sir Spencer Ponsonby-Fane, our first Governor and the last surviving founder, died at the age of ninety-one. He had been a deeply loved, if autocratic ruler and his interest in the club had never flagged. As recently as 1913 he had presided at the meeting of the Biennial Committee at Lord's; only in 1914 had his health prevented him from coming up. IZ cricket stopped at the outbreak of war. As Sir Spencer's successor, the Sixth Earl of Dartmouth, wrote later:

> There was no cricket. Cricket grounds and pavilions were given up to national needs. The Rolls of Honour lengthened as the days went by, and on top of all came the news that our beloved Governor had passed away. It was a shattering blow. It almost seemed as though our sun had set, and the time had come to haul down our flag and put up our shutters. We had three alternatives. We could close down. We could reorganise as an ordinary club; or we could endeavour to carry on on the old lines. We adopted the third course, believing that by so doing we should be best fulfilling the desire of the late Governor. It was an uphill task. We had to begin *de novo*.

How thankful we are now that this decision was taken!

Sir Spencer had some time before his death expressed a hope that Lord Dartmouth would be his successor and naturally the wish was respected. Though Lord Dartmouth had not been in the eleven at Eton, he had represented four second-class counties and had been invited to appear for a fifth, Devon, on apparently no other qualification than that he took his title from a town within its boundaries. He had played constantly for MCC and had captained the House of Commons side. He was immensely keen and cricket had played an important part in a busy life. On his first appearance at Lord's, for MCC *v.* Huntingdonshire in 1870, *Scores and Biographies* described him as 'a good average bat, slow round-arm bowler and in the field is generally long-stop'. He is said to have been a notable exponent of the Harrow drive, hit with tremendous power over cover's head and going first bounce into the boundary. He was President of MCC in 1893 and a Trustee from 1916 to his death, President of Kent in 1888 and for forty years President of Staffordshire. He had been a Conservative MP from 1878 to 1891, when he succeeded to the earldom, and Chamberlain of the Household from 1885 to 1892. He had a great sense of humour and also possessed the gift of being able to produce a set of verses at will on almost any current topic. One of his hobbies was acting and he was a great supporter of the Old Stagers. Moreover, he proudly claimed to be the only male Girl Guide. As Sir Pelham Warner wrote after his death, 'His great charm of manner, knowledge of men and matters and kindly disposition radiated happiness, and everywhere he was held in great esteem and affection.' A specimen of his 'occasional' verse may be given:

Mr. Arthur Balfour having accused Mr. Ure of a frigid and calculated lie, Mr. Byles raised the question in the House of Commons, and was told by the Speaker it would be best to leave the matter alone.

> To inquisitive Byles comes the Speaker's reply:
> 'It is better for us to let sleeping dogs lie'
> From this we may gather, its order to keep,
> The House much prefers to let lying dogs sleep.

When in 1932 IZ tied with Lords and Commons captained by Sir Rowland Blades, later Lord Ebbisham, himself a Zingaro, Lord Dartmouth sent him a present of an IZ tie, 'a tie for a tie match'. Innumerable letters show the enormous interest he took in every aspect of the club.

In August, 1918, the Freedom of IZ, which had hitherto been largely confined to the Lords Lieutenant of Ireland, who had entertained IZ sides at the Vice-Regal Lodge, was offered to Lord Beatty, Lord Jellicoe, Lord French and Lord Haig. All four gratefully accepted. Their letters are too long to quote, but a sentence from Lord Jellicoe's may be given, 'I can conceive no higher honour than to be thought worthy of admission into the ranks of the splendid company of sportsmen who are included under the name of I Zingari, whose principles are so fine and whose performances during the war have so fully acted up to those principles.' Lord French, one of whose sons was for years a prominent Zingaro, admitted that 'it was one of the greatest ambitions of my early youth to belong to IZ'. The same was true of Lord Montgomery, an ex-Captain of the St Paul's School XI, who was appointed a Freeman in 1967.

At a meeting of the Biennial Committee in February 1919, it was decided 'to renew active operation on a moderate scale'. Eventually twelve matches were arranged, six against schools and six against service sides. The highlight was a two-day 'Victory Match' against the Household Brigade at Lord's and 'there was a strong expression of opinion that the IZ side should be captained in the field by Lord Harris with the advice and encouragement of the Governor from the pavilion'. The match duly took place and IZ won by eight wickets. The scorecard read:

I ZINGARI

Cdr. G. H. D'O Lyon	c Jefferson b Cartwright	14	b Hughes	32
Cdr. C. F. R. Cowan	c Fitzgerald b Hambro	25	b Jefferson	22
M. Falcon	l.b.w., b Erskine	36		
J. N. Buchanan	run out	11		
P. R. Johnson	c Wilkinson b Cartwright	64	not out	2
G. E. V. Crutchley	c Brierly b Hambro	18		
Lord Harris	b Maitland	0		
Major F. R. R. Brooke	c Brierly b Hambro	4		
H. C. McDonell	b Cartwright	6		
R. H. Twining	not out	39	not out	3
P. W. Cobbold	b Cartwright	17		
	Byes	15	Byes 4, wide 1	5
		249		64

	O	M	R	W		O	M	R	W
Hambro	23	5	81	3					
Cartwright	18	1	82	4		7	0	11	0
Erskine	7	0	22	1					
Jefferson	7	1	29	0		6	1	31	1
Maitland	6	1	20	1		1.1	1	1	0
					Hughes	2	0	16	1

HOUSEHOLD BRIGADE

A. C. Wilkinson	c Cobbold b Falcon	0	b Cobbold	30
R. H. V. Cavendish	b Falcon	0	b Falcon	23
I. D. Erskine	c Brooke b Falcon	6	b Cobbold	2
Major G. H. M. Cartwright	b Cobbold	1	b Cobbold	8
J. Jefferson	b Falcon	0	b Cobbold	17
C. J. Hambro	l.b.w. b Cobbold	0	c Brooke b Cobbold	21
P. H. Fitzgerald	c Brooke b Falcon	2	b Cobbold	0
Capt. J. Hughes	b Cobbold	14	st Twining b McDonell	11
Major T. L. C. Curtis	b Falcon	18	c Johnson b Cobbold	2
Major M. Maitland	not out	7	not out	73
H. J. R. Brierly	l.b.w. b Cobbold	5	b Buchanan	43
	Byes 6, leg-byes 4	10	Byes 18, no-ball 1	19
		63		249

	O	M	R	W	O	M	R	W
Falcon	11	2	38	6	8	1	29	1
Cobbold	10.3	5	15	4	26	8	67	7
Buchanan					14	0	43	1
McDonell					10.5	0	49	1
Crutchley					6	0	20	0
Lyon					4	1	22	0

No fault could be found with the IZ side, although F. S. Jackson had to refuse his invitation: all of them had either played for a first-class county or had a blue, several were still playing for their counties when available and one, Michael Falcon (who was absent on the second day owing to parliamentary duties), had just represented the Gentlemen at Lord's and two years later bowled out the Australians for A. C. MacLaren's side at Eastbourne. Apart from Lord Harris, who was sixty-eight, only Cobbold, a Cambridge blue of 1896, was over forty, and it will be seen that his leg-breaks were highly effective. An account of the match says that he bowled them 'a great deal better than anything of the kind seen at Lord's this year'. Lord Harris, who was still well capable of getting runs, received 'the one ball of the innings which fizzed off the generally easy-paced pitch: it also broke back perceptibly. A modern player might have saved his stumps with his pads: the old-fashioned back stroke was a trifle late.' One further extract: 'It was no mean catch which dismissed Johnson. He hit a drive fair and square at mid-on's face. Wilkinson took the ball with one hand only, part of his right hand being somewhere in France.'

Many of us will remember with admiration how wonderfully Alex Wilkinson surmounted his handicap both in batting and fielding. It should be added that Maitland and Brierly were not, in fact, the last pair in the second innings: from the account it appears that their stand was for the eighth wicket, but the batting order is not given.

During this period two categories of members disappeared from the lists, 'Agents' and 'Members unattached to Cricket, but attached to IZ'. Agents were members appointed to promote the interests of the club in particular areas or communities and were allowed to play against IZ for their Agency, but not for other sides: a soldier might play against the club for his regiment, but not for the Aldershot Command or in a country-house match. Naturally a large number of the Agents were soldiers. In 1909 it had been decided that naval members should in future be Agents in order to enable them to play for the RN against IZ. With the abolition of Agents the rules were modified to enable members of the services to play for service sides against the club. The rule had not been enforced in matches against the Houses of Parliament since 1897.

'Members Attached to IZ' (the words 'unattached to Cricket' had been deleted in 1908) seem, though they included some good players, to have been elected primarily as a compliment or for services rendered to the club. It was for instance under this heading that those who had received the Freedom were entered. In the 1929 book a much reduced list of Attachés appears: by 1935 the names were all merged into the three categories which still exist. In 1981 it was decided to revive this category and Rose Leigh Pemberton was appointed an Attachée.

For many years there was also appended a list of 'Dependable Drags and Drivers'. They were not a separate category: their names also appeared elsewhere. They were men who in the pre-motor days could provide lifts for their friends to matches. They are commemorated thus in the 1929 book:

'Dependable Drags and Drivers' – an extinct race. They are no more. The last survivor long ago drove his final stage. There is no one to succeed them. Mechanical transport has taken the place of the drags and the teams. We are all drivers today. Are we dependable? For an answer I must refer you to the heads of our County Police Stations, who carefully and considerately keep our records for us.

A notable occasion was a dinner at the Mansion House on 26 March 1929, given to members by the Lord Mayor, Sir Kynaston Studd, the eldest of three brothers who played together in the Cambridge side and captained it in successive years, as did the Ashtons forty years later. This was, in accordance with the practice of the day, a more ceremonious affair than our modern dinners – the dress was white tie with the IZ sash (which now appears only on Epilogue Night in Canterbury Week), the IZ song* was sung, quite beautifully, it is said, by the principal Post-Prandial Precentor, R. H. Kennerley Rumford, and there were no less than seven speeches. Some 250 members attended.

In 1920 a match was played against the Rhine Army at Cologne and in the summer of 1923 General Sir Charles Harington, a Zingaro then commanding the Army of the Black Sea, arranged five matches for IZ in Turkey against service sides, of which four were won and one lost. The first of these was, if Wisden may be trusted, played on 31 June, a not inappropriate date for a club whose rules were drawn up 'at a Meeting held no matter when, and much less where'. In these matches a couple of hundreds were scored by Sir Michael Dillwyn-Venables-Llewelyn, for so many years one of the mainstays of the Household Brigade's batting.

One match in this period is still remembered by the survivors for a remarkable exhibition of bowling. IZ were playing the Aldershot Command and the side was collected by Willie Clark, who had given up playing himself but was umpiring, as he often did, and was thus able to see and hear all that passed on the field. Harry Altham was captaining the IZ side, which also included Rockley Wilson. Now Rockley after the Great War was content in club, as well as in first-class cricket, to be regarded solely as a bowler and to go in ten or eleven; so a generation had grown up which did not realize what a good bat he had been – one who had made a hundred in his first first-class match, a hundred in the Varsity match and a hundred for Yorkshire. On this occasion he had for some reason gone in earlier than he generally did and was making some runs. As usual he was scoring particularly well off his legs, where his technique was always impeccably correct: he was also a fine on-driver. Presently a rather moderate leg-break bowler was put on. He arranged his field carefully and, when he had finished, his captain said, 'I don't think you really

* At this period committee meetings always began with the song.

need that mid-wicket, do you?' The bowler looked at Rockley and said, 'Better keep him here for this farmyard player.' Rockley was not a man easily or often roused, but if there was one thing more than another which used to anger him, it was a breach of manners or etiquette, especially on the cricket field from someone who should have known better. He was certainly roused on this occasion. When IZ took the field, he declined the new ball, but the moment his enemy appeared bustled up to Harry and said, 'I think I'd like a go now, Harry, if I may.' What followed was described by Willie as the most extraordinary bowling he had ever seen. The batsman was a highly competent club and minor-county player, but Rockley was still probably the most accurate bowler in the world and for half an hour or more kept on just missing the off stump, just missing the edge of the bat, and, as he walked back, Willie could hear him muttering to himself, 'Farmyard player! Farmyard player!' At last one of the fielding side said as they were crossing over, 'Rockley, I don't think I've ever seen a bowler have such bad luck.' 'Bad luck! Bad luck! Keep the little bastard there another half-hour. Make him look a fool! Make him look a fool!'

While fixtures against service sides and schools continued much as before, the First World War had almost killed country-house cricket. Indeed I can remember that remarkable character, Gerry Weigall, a loyal Zingaro, saying to me in 1940 that he thought that after the war IZ should be disbanded because this type of cricket, which had formed such a large proportion of its programme in the old days, no longer existed. The only country-house matches I can trace IZ playing between the wars were two at Highclere, where the opposition and entertainment were provided by M. R. Aird, who lived at Woolton hard by, father of our present Treasurer, two against Sir John Power's XI at Newlands Manor and one at Badminton against the Beaufort Hunt. It was here that Henry Hunloke had to rush from the wicket when batting to intercept his car, which was seen careering downhill towards the lake, the brake having been released by Audley Miller, in whom sixty years had not quenched a passion for practical jokes.

Another change was a great reduction in the number of two-day matches. By 1939 IZ had only five, though other clubs still had plenty and it was easy, if one wished, to play three two-day matches a week from late July to early September. In earlier days Rockley Wilson's reason for refusing to play for Yorkshire for eleven years was that, with only some six weeks free for playing, he got more cricket by playing three two-day matches than two three-day ones. In any case the IZ season in the 1930s tended to end very early (in 1939 for instance on 5 August), so that schoolmasters had little opportunity of playing for the club and very few were appointed, thus depriving us of a valuable link with the schools. In some other clubs there was a different risk – that in August a side might well contain eight or nine schoolmasters on holiday. This recalls another story of Rockley, playing for the Quidnuncs in his last year at Cambridge.

Someone asked, 'What are you going to do, Rockley, when you've gone down?'

'I'm going to become a schoolmaster, really.'

'What a pity! Only takes two years of that to turn a good chap into a stinker.'

'There were,' said Rockley, 'nine schoolmasters in that dressing room.'

Between the wars a change was made in the status of Sibenes. In the old days they had been sons of friends of the Governor. They often became Sibenes very young: the 1895 book shows among them Lord Lewisham, our future Governor, aged fourteen, his younger brother aged thirteen and H. F. E. Somerset and M. A. T. Ridley, both aged nine. They were entitled to wear the colours and remained candidates till, at about the usual age, 'without further ceremony they passed on to become Members'. Now it was decided to make 'the candidature really probative', as it has remained ever since, and, as great care is taken in the selection of Sibenes, it is comparatively seldom that one fails to pass the test, unless, as sometimes happens, he has been negligent about playing for the club. Nor are they, not being members, entitled to wear the colours. When this rule first came in, the authorities had failed to lay down that they might wear other colours when playing for IZ and it was several years before this omission was rectified. Meanwhile some conscientious managers had refused to allow them to wear any colours at all. Lord Nugent could remember in his first IZ match being refused permission to wear his Eton Ramblers sweater as an alternative to pneumonia. Miles Howell, who, perhaps because he wore spectacles, always played in a cap and who had trousers which required a sash to keep them up, was refused both cap and sash. So he fielded holding up his trousers with one hand and, when he received a high catch into the sun, peered at it under his disengaged hand, released the other at the psychological moment and held the ball just as his trousers descended round his ankles. Miles was then thirty, had served throughout the war, captained Oxford at cricket and soccer, won an amateur international cap and could command a place in the very strong Surrey batting side whenever he was free to play. He was never a keen Zingaro.

Nor was he the only member disenchanted with the club. Its prestige was still great and plenty of young and good players were elected. They were proud to belong to it and to wear the colours, but after a few matches many decided that they would sooner play for other clubs. The trouble was that too many IZ match managers were far too old. In those days the average age of club and indeed of county sides was much higher than it is now. There was a far larger proportion of players over forty. Even in county cricket there were a few over fifty: in club cricket there were many. Further, in club cricket there were always some over sixty and an occasional one over seventy. Many of these veterans could still bat well and some were still very useful bowlers, but inevitably they were static in the field and were unlikely to be able to bowl above medium pace. Moreover, while there were many among them whom those of us who learned their cricket in those days remember with gratitude and affection, there was a limit to the number that a side could successfully assimilate, and as one of these elderly managers was almost sure to enlist some of his friends to bear him company and as the young tended to be shy of applying to them for places, IZ became a by-word for producing sides of elderly non-benders who might draw a match but were unlikely to win it, and who were not much fun to play with or against. There were also among them too many who regarded it as their duty to bring up the young the hard way and teach them to mind their *P*s and *Q*s, and the young at that time were often not newly left schoolboys but men who had fought in the war. Even schoolboys could find some of these sides oppressive. Raymond Robertson-Glasgow used to relate how he was bowling for Charterhouse against an elderly Zingaro, a player in his day of great distinction, who whenever a ball beat him used to call out loudly and pompously, though doubtless with the kindest intentions, 'Well bowled, boy.' Presently a ball from Raymond scattered his stumps, and there was a loud cry from mid-on, 'Well bowled, boy.' This was thought to be not well received.

A glance at the fixture cards and the scores is instructive. In 1921 the ages of the match managers ranged from sixty-two to thirty-five and their average age was forty-seven. The corresponding figures for 1981 are a range of forty-six to twenty-four and an average age of thirty-five. Taking a match in 1921 almost at random, the average age of the IZ side against West Kent was forty-four. There was one player, Lord Harris, of seventy (he made 50 not out), another, Captain E. G. Wynyard, of sixty, two more of over fifty, one of forty-nine and only one under thirty. It was a one-day match and IZ declared at 287 for 7. West Kent, who finished at 184 for 7, seem to have been saved from defeat by some spirited hitting by Jack Capes, a hockey international who later did useful work for Kent as a slow left-hander: going in at number nine he was 44 not out at the close. Wynyard took three wickets with his lobs and one is left wondering whether the unusual spectacle can have been witnessed of him and Lord Harris sharing the bowling with underhands.

Ronny Aird remembers playing against Lymington in 1926. He never rated himself as more than a change but found himself opening the IZ bowling with Christopher Heseltine. Thirty years before as a fast bowler, Heseltine had caused considerable trouble to the great Bobby Abel: at fifty-seven he was neither fast nor formidable. Lymington, having failed to score fast enough by the statutory time to declare, batted all the first day, IZ all the second. The fixture was not renewed. On one occasion when IZ were playing Winchester two boys were hopelessly stranded in the middle of the pitch, but the wicketkeeper, a veteran of over fifty, fumbled a good return from long leg and tripped over the stumps, so they escaped. Rockley Wilson's comment was, 'Been a bit unlucky to be run out from long leg playing against IZ, really.' Cosmo Crawley can remember in his first IZ match not only acting as runner for that great batsman Alec Johnston, who, grievously wounded in the First World War, could no longer run for himself and who on this occasion made, as he so often did, a hundred, but also fielding for a long time in the deep at both ends. He admits that, being young and keen, he enjoyed it, but such sides do not help the reputation of a club. Those were the days when Gerald Hough, himself a Zingaro and a good and shrewd cricketer, used to say that when batting he took a run automatically to anyone wearing IZ colours. No batsman following that principle in these days would last long.

It was not till about 1930 that the Committee took the essential step of appointing younger match managers. I have always understood that the prime movers in this were Billy Findlay, who had succeeded F. E. Lacey as Secretary, and Willie Clark, for so many years our Custos Rotulorum, though I cannot help suspecting that our present Treasurer, who has now been an officer of the club for over fifty years, had a hand in it, even if he is too modest to say so. Certainly he was himself one of the younger managers. These soon persuaded their contemporaries to play and I can only say, speaking for myself, that I found my IZ cricket in the 1930s most enjoyable. There might be a veteran or two on the side, as there then was in any other club, but usually he was a veteran who was worth his place, and the fielding in general was of a perfectly reasonable standard. Indeed the best club side on which I ever played was an IZ one.

It was that which George Kemp Welch took down to Charterhouse in 1938: the players' ages are given in brackets. Nigel Haig (fifty-one) had now given up county cricket after playing for Middlesex for twenty-five years, during which he had played often for the Gentlemen and once for England; he would no longer have bowled a first-class side out, but he could still put the ball where he wanted; no boy was going to get easy runs off him and he himself might well have made a hundred. Lionel Isherwood (forty-seven) was certainly not a great bat, but he had made runs in his time for both Hampshire and Sussex and as he played most days in the summer and had nets on the others, he was always in practice. Gubby Allen (thirty-six) had captained the England side on the last tour in Australia and might well have done so in England that summer had not an injury, which prevented him from bowling in this match, put him out of the running. George Kemp Welch (thirty-one) had captained Cambridge, gone in first for the Gentlemen at Lord's and played for Warwickshire when they could get him. Giles Baring (twenty-eight) had missed a blue at Cambridge but had the satisfaction of taking 9 for 26 for Hampshire *v.* Essex while the Varsity match was being played at Lord's, and had bowled out the 1934 Australians at Southampton. He was still, despite a bad car smash, really fast and could make the ball run away, and was still also playing for Hampshire when he could. Holcombe Read (twenty-eight) had played for England in 1935, when he was the fastest bowler in the country: he had now given up county cricket, moderated his pace and increased his accuracy, but he was still faster than many batsmen cared to play. Arthur Hazlerigg (twenty-eight) had captained Cambridge and Leicestershire and played for the Gentlemen: he was a good bat and his slow off-spin had caused trouble to Oxford at Lord's. Roger Winlaw (twenty-six), whose son has been so prominent in IZ cricket in recent years, had played three years for Cambridge, and made his fair share of runs for Surrey after term was over. Michael Tufnell (twenty-two) kept wicket that year for the Navy.

The match was twelve-a-side and the team was completed by three humble club cricketers (aged thirty-two, twenty-one and twenty-one), two of whom were Sibenes. The school, who had a strong side, were naturally defeated, but were by no means disgraced. Some of them indeed, emerged with considerable credit. In collecting a side like this George had in mind not only the depressing IZ teams which he and I remembered from our schooldays at Charterhouse, but also how little cricket we had ever been taught or had had the chance of learning. He himself, good player though he later became, had in his last year a batting average of 8. I still treasure a letter he wrote me when Sir Robert Birley was appointed Headmaster in 1935. 'I hope the new Headmaster will ensure that Carthusians are taught not to play forward to the quick off-spinner bowled at a length for the sheer joy of having their leg-stump knocked out.' This was of course written before the disastrous effects of the new l.b.w. law had become apparent. Nor had George realized that Wilfrid Timms, with the help of Bob Relf, had revolutionized Charterhouse cricket and put it firmly on the right lines.

On 11 March 1936, Lord Dartmouth died at the age of eighty-four and was succeeded as Governor by his son, the Seventh Earl. He, like his father, had not been in the eleven at Eton, but he had captained Christ Church and was a member of the Authentics. He had been President of the Kent County Cricket Club in 1925 and had the doubtful privilege of being President of MCC at the time of the body-line controversy. During the First World War he served in Palestine with the Staffordshire Yeomanry, which he later commanded. At that time he was MP for West Bromwich. Losing his seat in the election immediately after the war, he farmed for many years at Godmersham, in Kent, but moved to London on being appointed Lord Great Chamberlain. He had been Master of the Christ Church Beagles and was a very good shot and fisherman. Unlike his father he had played little IZ cricket and felt himself ill-qualified to express opinions on the game, but the club meant much to him and in handing over to his successor, he spoke of the governorship as 'what I believe to be the happiest experience cricket can give'. He possessed great charm and a dry sense of humour and the Committee meetings held at his house in London were memorable for his generous hospitality and, in particular, for the lunch which preceded them. It is true that at these meetings the younger members of the Committee tended to feel that they were expected to be seen rather than heard, and that discussions and decisions were really the province of their elders. But if in this respect things are, rightly, very different now, this is a change which is common to society in general and not peculiar to IZ.

R. L. ARROWSMITH

7

1945–81

DURING the Second World War IZ lay dormant, but in 1946, as in 1919, a tentative start was made with eleven days' cricket. Next year the number was increased to twenty and from this it has slowly crept up to thirty-three days, about the same as in 1939. Throughout we have been careful to take on new matches only when we were confident of sufficient support, and where we have found that a fixture does not attract applications, we have dropped it or altered the venue. For instance members did not show enthusiasm for driving down a crowded road on a Saturday or Sunday to play a one-day match at Chatham against our old friends the Sappers, or even further in the same direction to play BB at Canterbury. We now play the Sappers at Aldershot and, thanks to the kindness of Robin and Rose Leigh Pemberton, BB on one day of a weekend at Torry Hill and both matches are well subscribed. Above all we have avoided enlarging our fixture list to an extent which would necessitate increasing our membership and lowering our standards.

Inevitably after seven years when no new members had been elected there were some teething troubles in the first season or two, but the mistake of having elderly match managers was not repeated and soon young and reasonably good sides became the rule rather than the exception. Ian Fleming, running an IZ match for the first time in 1946, still remembers that it was impressed on him that he must produce a good fielding side, an injunction which he faithfully observed as long as he managed the match.

In the last thirty-five years a considerable change has taken place in the fixture list. The school matches remain what they always have been, but the two-day matches against service sides, with the splendid evenings in the mess on the first day, have completely vanished, one fears for ever. The reason is of course that the radical changes in the conditions of service life make it impossible for our opponents to offer hospitality on the old scale or, for the most part, to produce sides of the old standard. Another sad casualty is the matches against Oxford and Cambridge colleges. These continued with increasing difficulty to the end of the 1960s, by which time it had become clear that the colleges could no longer raise adequate opposition and, indeed, were sometimes unable to collect a side at all. As against this, there has been one surprising and welcome development. In 1939 IZ did not play a single day's cricket on anything that could possibly be described as a country-house ground. In 1981 they had fourteen such days, all in delightful surroundings. When one considers the effort and expense required to maintain such grounds in these days, one cannot be sufficiently grateful to those who make it possible, whether they be private individuals or clubs like the Hampshire Hogs.

A hundred years ago IZ played all over England, regularly toured Ireland and sometimes appeared in Scotland. Now the great majority of matches are within fifty or sixty miles of London and, when we go farther afield, to Wylam for instance or Crickhowel, most of our side are still drawn from the Southeast. Even for our matches in the Midlands we get comparatively little help from members living locally, many of whom are likely in any case to be playing for our opponents. In 1970 rule 8, which strictly forbade members to play against the club, was suspended *sine die*. For some years the Governor had had to sanction an increasing number of exemptions from this rule if our hosts were to raise adequate sides and it seemed farcical to retain it. It could have continued to work only if we had refrained from electing to IZ members of the opposition, and to this the objections are obvious. With the astronomical rises in the price of petrol, the problem is steadily getting worse; there is no obvious answer, but one would certainly not wish IZ to become, if not a suburban, at least a Southeastern club. Such was far from being the intention of our founders.

Nor have IZ since the Second World War played outside the United Kingdom. The late Governor, while Governor-General of New Zealand, was anxious that an IZ side should go out there and Rothmans were prepared to subsidize the scheme, but it was felt that IZ of all clubs ought not to accept sponsorship for playing cricket. To accept, as we have now done most gratefully, the very generous sponsorship of Hambros in the production of this book is a different matter: we were founded for the encouragement of purely amateur cricket, but the publication of books was never envisaged as one of our objects. A five-day tour of Holland arranged for 1967 unfortunately fell through.

After the Second World War as after the First the Freedom of the club was offered to four who had rendered distinguished service to the nation, Sir Winston Churchill, Lord Cunningham, Lord Alanbrooke and Lord Portal, who had in fact been in the Winchester XI, but played little cricket afterwards. All honoured the club by acceptance. Since then it has been bestowed on Lord Montgomery of Alamein; on Sir Robert Menzies, a tremendous supporter of cricket in Australia and, when his office as Warden of the Cinque Ports brought him to England, in this country as well; on our present Governor, who was then our Prime Minister and who had been a valuable playing member in his active days; on the Duke of Norfolk, who entertained us so superbly at Arundel and did so much for cricket in other ways, and later on his widow, Lavinia, Duchess of Norfolk, to whose generosity and determination the survival of cricket at Arundel is largely due; on Lord Chandos, a member of one of our greatest Zingaric families and himself a Zingaro with a distinguished record in public life; on Sir William Worsley, an ex-Captain of Yorkshire, who entertained IZ for years at Hovingham, and on his daughter, the Duchess of Kent, who is remembered with gratitude and affection by all who played there; on two distinguished soldiers, both Zingari and both good Army cricketers in their day, Field Marshal Sir James Cassels and General Sir Neil Ritchie; on Gubby Allen, a great ex-Captain of England, sometime Chairman of the Selectors and Treasurer of MCC, who had also often done good service in the past for the club as a player; on Lord Cornwallis, a notable figure both at Lord's and in Kent, where he had captained the county side; and on four whose services to the club off the field, let alone on it, have been outstanding, Brigadier Willie Clark, Sir John Masterman, Cosmo Crawley and Ronny Aird, who has been first our Secretary and later our Treasurer for over fifty years. Apart from the work he has done in these capacities, his infinite wisdom has been of incalculable value to IZ on many occasions.

In 1956 Lord Dartmouth, feeling that he could no longer keep sufficiently in touch with the younger generation and also that he had the ideal successor at hand, resigned and was succeeded as Governor by the Tenth Viscount Cobham, who as the Hon. Charles Lyttelton had captained Worcestershire from 1936 to 1939. The new Governor had had a cricket career to which one could find few parallels. At Eton it seemed that he had inherited hardly any of the exceptional gifts of his family. He was nowhere near the XI and when after leaving he began to play for BB and Butterflies, one felt that his main claim to a place was his name. But he was keen and determined, he studied the theory of the game intensely, he was monumentally strong and he obviously had in fact more natural ability than he had been credited with. I was lucky enough to play much with him in the next few years and to form a friendship which ended only with his death.

It was fascinating to watch his development. Before he came down from Cambridge, he had been summoned to the nets at Fenner's and had been awarded a Crusader. I well remember his first century in any kind of cricket, 132 not out for Butterflies *v.* St Lawrence at Canterbury in 1931; it included a drive over the vast and repulsive concrete stand to the south of the pavilion. Off the previous ball he had made an even harder hit, the ball striking the top rim of the stand while still rising. I was batting with him at Tunbridge Wells when he cleared the pavilion and there was a crash of broken glass behind. We met in the middle of the pitch and roared with laughter: a few minutes later he got out and found that he had shattered the windscreen of his own brand-new Austin. It was in 1932 that he first appeared for Worcestershire and after playing a good deal in the next three seasons and going as Vice-Captain with Erroll Holmes's MCC team to New Zealand in 1935–6, he took over the captaincy in 1936. Wisely he adhered to the tactics which had served him so well in club cricket; though he did not neglect the art of defence and was prepared, if wanted, to open the innings, he still believed that the best form of defence was attack, especially on a bad wicket or against a good bowler. Against the Australians in 1938 he scored 50 and 35, going in first and being especially severe on O'Reilly, then the finest bowler in the world. In 1936 when Worcestershire, playing Yorkshire on an impossible wicket, beat them for the first time since 1909, it was his first innings of 48 in thirty-five minutes that made victory possible. It was innings such as these, quite apart from his shrewd and inspiring captaincy, that made him well worth his place in a side which by 1939 he had raised to seventh in the championship. Sometimes he played a longer innings: his highest and his only century was 162 against Leicestershire in 1938. After the war he confined himself to club cricket and was still an active and dangerous player when he became Governor; he even found time to continue the game when Governor-General of New Zealand from 1957 to 1962. Indeed the climax of his career came when in 1961, at the age of fifty-one, he captained his own side at Auckland against the MCC touring team and made 44 in twenty-one minutes, including two sixes.

Since cricket had played so great a part in his life and provided him with many of his happiest memories, he regarded it as his duty (and a very pleasant one) to do all he could for the game and especially for that form of it which he had particularly enjoyed, the cricket played by wandering clubs. Apart from his work for IZ, he was for twenty-five years Captain of the Butterflies, whose Kent tours in his Cambridge days he always felt had helped enormously in his development. For some years he was also Chairman of the Free Forester Committee. In addition to this he had been President and later Treasurer of MCC and only a few days before his death had become President of Worcestershire. Nor in any of these posts or in the countless other responsibilities he assumed was he content to be a mere figurehead; in all he took a lively and active interest. Even from New Zealand he kept a watchful eye on IZ and after his return it can never have been long out of his thoughts. His innumerable commitments in Worcestershire at weekends stopped him from getting round to watch our matches as much as he would have liked, but his correspondence about the club in general and about candidates must have been enormous. I have a vast file of letters from him, all written in his own beautiful copperplate hand and often covering both sides of two or three large sheets. Many started with some matter connected with IZ and then would range over a variety of subjects: cricket in general, English or classical literature, anything, indeed, in which I shared his interest. Like his uncle, George, whom he so greatly admired, he was in the tradition of the great eighteenth-century letter-writers: letter-writing to him was an art and a relaxation. With him in the chair no meeting could be dull and, if at times his flow of reminiscences prolonged the session somewhat, one never felt that any item had failed to receive due attention. He was himself a very wise counsellor.

Mention too must be made of his hospitality to the club. Between 1970 and 1976 IZ played six matches at Hagley, three of them two-day ones at which they were put up. Their opponents were the Flamingos, the Toronto CC, Hagley Village, and on two occasions the London New Zealand CC, who played again under the new regime in 1981. There was also a notable inter-IZ match, Match Managers *v.* The Governor's XI. The parties in particular held for the two-day matches will be long remembered. With eight children of his own the Governor had no difficulty in bridging the 'generation gap', a phrase which in any case he regarded as ridiculous and harmful. He was immensely appreciative of the kindness and friendliness of the modern young and if, as a party went on, the fun waxed fast and furious, one who had in his own undergraduate days been on such occasions always to the forefront felt no inclination to resent or repress it. In his will he left a handsome legacy to IZ hoping it might encourage others to follow his example.

It was in 1954 that IZ, after an interval of many years, played again on one of those country-house grounds which were once regarded almost as the natural setting for our cricket and which now, by a most unexpected and welcome change of fortune, have become once more a feature of our programme. Thanks to the de Rothschilds, who have throughout been most generous in their hospitality, an IZ side managed by Alastair McCorquodale, whose eminence as an Olympic sprinter tends to make people forget that he had a trial for Middlesex as a fast bowler, played for three seasons the Whaddon Chase Hunt at Ascott, near Wing. This was replaced by a match against the de Rothschilds' XI, which continued till 1964, and then after a long gap we played there again for three seasons against Peter Stoddart's XI. In 1981 this fixture was exchanged for a match against the Harrow Wanderers. The ground is one on which till 1980 Buckinghamshire had a fixture annually and, though the wicket has been subject to those fluctuations from which even county and Test match wickets seem in these days never to be exempt, it has at its best been very good indeed. It is a singularly beautiful ground, bounded on two sides by glorious trees, which provide a welcome excuse for uncertain catchers, and on another, opposite the pavilion, affording a view of the Whaddon Chase Kennels and at times, if one is lucky, of hounds being exercised. In 1978 and 1979 we played there for two days, with a dance laid on for the Saturday night by Peter Stoddart, at which the enthusiasm and prowess of our Auditor was much admired.

In 1955 we were lucky enough to acquire two more country-house fixtures, at Hovingham, an account of which by John Tanner will be found later in this chapter, and at Highclere, where we have now been playing Lord Porchester's XI for twenty-five years, subject only to interruption by the weather. This is another beautiful ground, set in the midst of a park landscaped by Capability Brown and still remaining unaltered and unspoilt. For many years our host captained his side himself. Like all good hosts, he is always keen to win – and, indeed, what fun is cricket for either side if one isn't? – and he generally produces a team which takes a lot of beating. It is a very fast-scoring ground on which the timing of a declaration is notoriously tricky and we have had many splendid matches there. A victory there is something to be proud of.

In 1961 we first played on the ground that of all these is best known to the public, the Duke of Norfolk's ground at Arundel. Here again our host for some years captained his own side, contributing, as he would himself have been the first to admit, more enthusiasm than skill, but certainly enhancing everyone's pleasure by his own obvious enjoyment. He abhorred a draw and woe betide a team that was openly playing for one! In his lifetime, the hospitality was on a Victorian or Edwardian scale. Naturally that is no longer possible, but the privilege of being still able to play on a ground widely acclaimed as one of the loveliest in the world is in itself enough, and we owe an inestimable debt to the present Duke, who allows its use, to Lavinia, Duchess of Norfolk, our Freeman, who has refused to be daunted by the difficulty of keeping it going, and to all those who have helped her to do so. The only drawback of Arundel is that the wicket gives so little help to the bowler that the later batsmen on each side have little hope of getting to the wicket except in order to hit desperately to expedite a declaration or to win the match against the clock.

From 1968 we have played annually against Dick Hawkins's XI at Everdon Hall, Northants. Dick's father, who like himself was an MFH, was also a member of the county side in its early first-class days and there was cricket at Everdon up to the First World War. Like many others, the ground then fell out of use. It was restored by Dick after the Second World War and, thanks to many years of loving care by himself and others, is now a very good one. It differs from the other country-house grounds described in that it is less closely surrounded by trees. There are plenty of trees in sight and some particularly fine ones in the garden behind the hedge which forms part of the boundary, but they are farther from the wicket and so the light is better and there are views over much typical Northamptonshire hunting country. One might suppose that, standing high as it does, it would be a quick-drying ground, but in fact it is kept moist by springs and needs a spell of fine weather to be at its best. Though the match is played in July, it has not on the whole been favoured by the weather and on one occasion at least had to be abandoned without a ball being bowled. Dick has collected, especially in the earlier years, some formidable sides. He always seemed to be able to produce one or two of that invaluable type of bowler who, without looking deadly from the ring, will wheel away happily throughout an innings, always there or thereabouts, moving the ball just a trifle, giving nothing away and making it difficult for the batsmen to score runs at any reasonable pace. Indeed, it was not till 1975 that we recorded our first victory here, though in 1972 we had a tie, our host himself, if memory serves, being dismissed in what must have been the last over. In recent years some of the local stalwarts have dropped out, IZ has usually produced stronger sides and honours have been more evenly distributed. It is pleasant to record that our host still captains his sides himself, though it is many years since he could be persuaded to display those talents which earned him in his schooldays some reputation as a spinner of the ball. Since 1979 our debt to Dick has been increased by a second match at Everdon in September against J. H. Weatherby's XI, a fixture much patronized by the racing fraternity.

But perhaps the place where one feels nearest to the type of cricket played by IZ a century ago is Torry Hill, where we started with a match against the Eton Ramblers in 1973. From 1974 we have normally played three matches, the Eton Ramblers in May and a week-end in August, when we play BB and Robin Leigh Pemberton's XI, the sides on the Sunday differing only in two or three instances from those on the Saturday. Of the eight who founded BB in 1858, four were Pembertons, and the family has had an unbroken association with the club ever since. BB's first match was against a side from Torry Hill on Sir Courtenay Honeywood's ground at Evington. The return, some three weeks later, was played at Gore Court, Sittingbourne: presumably there was not then a suitable ground at Torry Hill. But when in 1879 Lord Harris revived BB, which had lain dormant for nine years, the first match was at Torry Hill itself, though not on the present ground, followed by another there two days later.

Lying in a beautiful and incredibly remote part of Kent, out of sight and sound of motorways, electrified lines and unsightly building developments, Torry Hill is difficult for the unlearned to find but is well worth the finding – one is in a setting which cannot look much different from what it did a hundred years ago. What is more, at the August weekend Robin and Rose Leigh Pemberton, incredibly, manage still to put up the IZ side and from snatches of conversation which one overhears on Sunday, the Saturday-night party is well in the traditions of a bygone age. Moreover, the friendliness and informality ensure that the shyest Sibene must feel perfectly at home from the moment he arrives, unlike some of the rather daunting country-house parties which the older among us can remember from our young days. Thanks largely to the work put into it by the family, the wicket has improved markedly in recent years and even a really fast bowler should not now cause a good-hearted player any qualms. If IZ's record in the August matches looks a trifle disappointing, the reason is an honourable one: we have uniformly produced good sides (the match is naturally very popular), but BB have produced even better ones. Speaking as one with a foot in both camps, who between the wars played much BB cricket and ran many BB sides, I never succeeded however hard I tried (and against the Harlequins and the Club and Ground I tried very hard indeed) in raising sides that could match, at any rate in bowling, those that Richard Gracey annually collects against IZ. In fact we have seen at Torry Hill year after year cricket of a very high standard.

Since 1973 IZ have played annually John Pawle's XI at Widford, near Ware. The ground was made in 1882 by John's grandfather, who when he bought the property in 1879 had two main requirements, 'a good cellar' and 'a level piece of land to lay a cricket square'. Both the cricket and the hospitality at Widford suggest that he got what he wanted and much good cricket has been played there during the last hundred years.

In our earlier matches two performances by Michael Hodgson stand out. In 1973 he was top scorer with 76 and in 1979 brought off a catch so sensational that it is still vividly remembered. Mike Hooper, as dangerous a bat as can be found in club cricket and a valued Zingaro, had opened the innings for the home side with five majestic fours in the first three overs and IZ feared the worst. At this point Hooper struck a fearsome hook off the middle of the bat and Hodgson leapt across behind the umpire to the right to hold the ball high above his head. The bowler, Fergus McMullen, doubtless encouraged by this, went on to take five wickets and in 1980 achieved the best figures recorded for IZ in this fixture, 7 for 53. The most exciting match in the series was in 1981. John Pawle's XI had declared at 210 for 9 and IZ, who at one time were 156 for 6, won by two wickets off the last ball of the match. They owed much to Mike Doggart, a Sibene of distinguished cricket lineage, who, having taken 3 for 31, went on to score 84.

In 1981 we played for the first time at Norwood Park, near Southwell, against Sir John Starkey's XI. Accounts speak highly both of the ground and of the hospitality we received. It sounds a welcome addition to our fixture list.

Two other grounds on which we play must not be left unsung, Wylam, which is no longer a country-house ground, and Warnford, which never was. Wylam, near Hexham, was before the war the private ground of the Bewickes and much good cricket used to be played there. Calverly Bewicke is himself a Zingaro. It has passed out of the Bewicke family, but now belonging to Newcastle University, is still maintained, and we played the Borderers there in 1978 and were entertained with true northern hospitality. It is particularly beautiful and has a larger playing area than most country-house grounds. Unfortunately a fixture arranged there for 1981 had to be cancelled.

Anyone seeing Warnford for the first time would suppose it to have been a country-house ground, but he would be wrong. Its history is a most encouraging one. As late as the Second World War it was a rough field used for folding pigs. After the war a rather primitive cricket ground was made there which, as Rex Chester, whose father farmed it, began to show enthusiasm and promise for the game, was improved and became the ground of the West Meon and Warnford Club. Later the Hampshire Hogs began to play matches there and, when the Chesters felt that they could no longer afford to maintain it, took it over from them on a lease in 1974 and have used it ever since as their home ground, enlarged it and built a handsome and comfortable pavilion. What is more, for several years they had no groundsman; the work was done by the members, and Jumbo Fuller, their Secretary, can remember motoring down the Meon valley at 5 a.m. to roll the wicket while the dew was still on it. It is a splendid saga of keenness and determination. Though the ground is only a hundred yards or so from the main road, it is surrounded by trees and fields and might be miles from anywhere. Moreover no fault can be found either with the wicket or the outfield.

We have now played the Hogs here since 1969. They have always, ever since I can remember, been an extremely friendly club and great fun to play against. To anyone who does not know the ground a visit, whether as player or spectator, can be highly recommended.

John Tanner gives the following account of IZ in Yorkshire.

'Between the years 1955 and 1973, I Zingari played four fixtures in Yorkshire, all within a radius of fifty miles from York. These were against Sir William Worsley's XI at Hovingham, the College at Ampleforth, Northern Command at Catterick and Yorkshire Gentlemen at Escrick Park.

If first mention goes to Hovingham, that is because its club has been connected with cricket for many generations and its ground in regular play for well over a century. There is a print showing a game in progress in 1837 and one old score book records a match in 1858 against All England, with such famous names as Julius Caesar and H. H. Stephenson, who captained the first English team to visit Australia in 1861. Both played for Surrey as well as All England.

Although seriously conducted, the cricket at Hovingham was incidental to the other pleasures of the day. It was essentially a country match, watched slumbrously under the shade of oak trees and against the background of Hovingham Hall, often to the strains of the local band, which on several occasions performed at the British Legion Garden Fête held simultaneously in the grounds. Hospitality was excellent, both during the game and afterwards, for which IZ owed much to the then Lady Worsley and her daughter, Katharine.

The first of eleven matches against Sir William's XI was played in 1955 and was distinguished by the appearance in the home team of Leonard Hutton. He had a field day, taking 5 for 43 and then making a rapid 77, to contribute largely to IZ's defeat by eight wickets.

Leonard Hutton was not available in 1956, but unfortunately for IZ, Brian Sellars and Don Brennan were. After IZ had made 204, these two helped knock off the runs for the loss of only five wickets, though the match was won only in the last over.

The 1957 fixture was ruined by rain and in 1958 a close finish resulted in a draw, with David Wilson making an excellent 50 for IZ.

In 1959, Sir William may have decided that it was once more time to stamp local authority on proceedings and Leonard Hutton again took the field. IZ batted first and made a solid 179, Hutton taking

0 for 53. But he then batted brilliantly, making 105 in 105 minutes and enabling Sir William's XI to win comfortably.

Of the remaining games, the 1960 match was drawn, IZ lost again in 1961, but won in both 1962 and 1963, due mainly to good and keen fielding, including the holding of some excellent catches. However, following a drawn match in 1964, Sir William's XI again won easily in 1965. At this point, Sir William, for many excellent reasons, decided to call it a day and the fixture was discontinued. All who played in it are extremely grateful for some happy memories and for warm hospitality received. All told, at Hovingham, IZ won two, lost five, drew three and one was abandoned.

It had been the custom to play at Hovingham on Saturday and Ampleforth on Sunday and it was possible for a while to replace the Saturday fixture at Hovingham by one against Northern Command at Catterick. Though the background was less rural, this was no less pleasant an occasion, laced with typical and friendly army hospitality. The IZ record over the period between 1967 and 1971 was three matches lost and two abandoned.

For the Ampleforth match, it was the custom to foregather at the Malt Shovel Inn at Oswaldkirk, preparatory to a midday start. We would subsequently motor along the Ampleforth ridge and down to the College ground, with its superb views south to the Howardian Hills. Of all the wickets on which we played, this was normally the fastest and certainly in direct contrast to the spongy conditions encountered down the valley at Hovingham. It called for rather more rapid adjustment than some were perhaps capable of achieving following the Saturday evening's entertainment. Whatever the reasons IZ seldom did itself justice at Ampleforth and won only three of nineteen matches. On the whole, the weather was the winner; only three contests were lost, thirteen being either drawn or abandoned. Needless to say, we were well looked after, with Benedictine hospitality and a traditional glass of port after lunch. A seat just to the left of the presiding priest was much prized!

The matches against Yorkshire Gentlemen, played at Escrick Park, about six miles south of York, between the years 1962 and 1971, did not form part of the Hovingham-Ampleforth-Catterick weekend and were an occasion apart. The ground itself lies to the southeast of what is now a well-known country-house school for girls in a most pleasant setting, with traditional park-like views on three sides. The demands of modern agriculture have more recently detracted from views to the south, which is now somewhat bereft of trees. Those who played recall generous hospitality and the record shows that IZ won only one match, four being lost, four drawn and one abandoned.

We have all been sorry to see these Yorkshire matches disappear and it would be very pleasant to think that at some point they could be resuscitated. This would not be practicable without an increase in the number of Zingari living in the area. There were about thirty more or less local players who could be called upon over the period in question, but this had dwindled to about twenty by 1973. Match managers found this an increasing nightmare and it became difficult to field a balanced side. But what fun the fixtures were and what a pity it will be if all IZ matches have to be confined to an area within immediate striking distance of London and the Home Counties! The remedy is partly in the club's own hands!'

Of IZ *v.* South Wales Hunts, Antony Winlaw writes:

'I Zingari played in Wales for the first time since the end of the Second World War in 1965, when a fixture was established against South Wales Hunts. The match was played in the village of Creigiau, and the club certainly "kept their wickets up" as reiterated by the Governor. IZ recorded the handsome total of 329 for 9 declared, with a Wykehamist trio of P. J. R. Scott (81), N. C. D. Craig (64) and V. A. L. Powell (48) as the leading batsmen.

The following year the match was transferred to the RAF Ground at St Athan. P. W. Gore, a left-arm spin bowler, took five wickets in each innings, and then that experienced batsman G. P. S. Delisle (71) brought IZ victory by eight wickets.

Since those two initial years the match has been played on the Welsh Regiment Ground, Cwrt Y Gollen, Crickhowel, and, on this classically easy-paced batting wicket, spoils have been evenly shared. IZ won three times in the first seven years, but not for a further ten years, during which the Hunts won three times, did the club triumph again – by 97 runs in 1981.

South Wales Hunts, whose membership was confined to "landowners, subscribers or supporters of one of the packs of foxhounds in South Wales", was founded in 1926. Their first President was Viscount Tredegar, and the joint Secretaries were G. L. Clay and L. E. W. Williams.

When IZ played them nearly "forty years on", the same "Tip"

Williams remained, a formidable figure in office, as Chairman. Another Clay – J. C. Clay, one of the most revered of all Welsh cricketers and a member of IZ – was now President. It was during the IZ match in 1973 that news came through of J. C. Clay's death, and our Governor, Lord Cobham, paid tribute to him before a minute's silence in the lunch interval. J. T. Morgan, the 1930 Cambridge Captain, who scored 149 in the 1929 University match, was later the Hunts' President, and was himself succeeded in 1977 by another Carthusian, I. E. Pugh.

I Zingari has enjoyed a marked contrast of success with bat and ball in Wales, with two batsmen especially prominent – M. J. J. Faber and D. A. J. Baldry.

Faber scored 108 and 59 as a Sibene in 1970, and the following season made 181 not out, with masterful cover-driving a feature of this highest innings in the fixure. He had a most able partner in R. C. Daniels (76), and 166 runs were added for the second wicket, in an IZ total of 294 for 3 declared. In the second innings Daniels scored another 50, whilst B. G. Brocklehurst merrily attacked for 87 runs, to help bring IZ another win by eight wickets.

Baldry's record alone tells the story of his sovereign batting in Wales. He scored a hundred in each of his first four appearances in the match (1975–9), to boast an aggregate of 589 runs at an average of 117.80. In 1979 Baldry (143 not out) enjoyed an undefeated second-wicket partnership of 170 runs with M. G. M. Groves (83 not out), and IZ declared at 263 for 1. But even after such an arrogant start, the club still failed to bowl the Hunts out in either innings.

I Zingari's bowlers have always had to strive hard for success against our opponents' determined batting, and much is owed to the loyal efforts of such as T. A. L. Huskinson, S. G. B. Burgess and R. S. Miller. In 1980 Ian Collett took six wickets for only 18 runs and the Hunts were dismissed for 78. But, yet again, there came frustration in the field as the Hunts batted throughout Sunday's play to draw the match at 230 for 6.

The club's best bowling exploit of all came in the second innings of 1981, and brought victory by 97 runs. R. A. Hutton was the determined body in a Hunts' collapse in the final hour (109 all out), and he finished with telling figures of 5 for 19 in eleven overs.

It was indeed appropriate that one of the members responsible for the long-awaited success in this match was S. G. Metcalfe. He and a Sibene, Philip Rudd, who scored an excellent 114 not out in a total of 235 for 4 declared, enjoyed a second wicket partnership of 109 on the first morning, and Metcalfe's innings of 59 brought his aggregate in this fixture past 1000 runs.

Metcalfe admittedly scored more of those runs for the Hunts than for IZ, as for the first ten years he played for the opposition. In 1972 he recorded their highest innings to date, with 109 runs. But then, after two years of match retirement, he was persuaded to change sides and return to Crickhowel. The IZ captain certainly valued his shrewd words of Yorkshire advice from first slip.

On completion of those 1000 runs Metcalfe duly re-announced his retirement. It was also the last year as captain for A. S. R. de W. Winlaw, who had managed IZ for seventeen years. In that time the Hunts themselves only fielded two captains – J. C. R. Downing and R. F. S. Miles – and one of the undoubted attractions of this match has been the annual meeting of familiar faces. Another feature of its success is the fine Welsh hospitality, with many a joyous party to relish on the Saturday evening – and many an excuse for all those unforeseen IZ failures on the second day's play in Wales!'

A notable event was the tour of England by IZ Australia in 1977. An account of this from their point of view appears later in this volume. From our point of view it was a great joy to meet them. To most of us, IZ Australia was only a name and we had known little about them and so we were delighted to find a club bearing our name and wearing our colours that so plainly upholds the principles on which we were founded, in an environment which we have always associated with cricket of a sterner and more serious nature. If we ever have the chance of paying them a return visit, we shall be proud if we can collect as charming a side as they sent to play us here.

On 20 March 1977, our Governor, Lord Cobham, died, sadly before his time, and the Committee unanimously decided to ask Lord Home of the Hirsel to succeed him. Already we owe him a great debt. Despite his many other commitments he has found time each season to watch a considerable number of our matches and he is probably known personally to a larger number of our active playing members than any of his predecessors. As Lord Dunglass, he had been a valuable all-rounder in the Eton XI of 1921 and 1922, had had trials for Oxford University, where he was elected a Harlequin, and for Middlesex, and was a member of the MCC side to the Argentine under Sir Pelham Warner in 1926–7. Later his political career restricted his cricket, but he was for years one of the mainstays of the Lords and Commons XI. He was a thorough cricketer, a fast-medium bowler who could swing the ball away and could extract some life from even the least responsive pitch, a fine catcher in the slips and a good practical batsman, who played straight and was particularly strong on the leg side and thus likely to get runs on slow wickets on which many of his companions were less successful. Against Harrow at Lord's in 1922, after rain had prevented any cricket on the Friday, he made 66, fairly easily top score, and followed it by taking 4 for 37.

We are no less fortunate in our Auditor, who also operates as our Secretary, modestly concealing his identity in that office, as have his predecessors, under the name of 'A. Secret'. The amount of work that he does for us and has been doing for nearly thirty years is incredible. His correspondence alone, in a hand which rivals in legibility that of our late Governor, must be enormous, and it is extraordinary with how many members, especially Full Play members, he contrives to keep in close contact. He has too been quite tireless in going round matches. What proportion of his time is devoted to IZ, one could not begin to estimate. The present book owes much to his help and interest.

Of our Treasurer, Ronny Aird, and his wonderful services to the club over more than fifty years mention has been made before. One may add that his annual presentation of the accounts to the Committee is an occasion eagerly awaited, a rare tribute. There is never a dull moment.

Under such guidance it is not surprising that IZ flourishes in a world very different from that in which it was founded and it does so without ever losing sight of the principles of our forefathers, principles which it is doubly important to uphold at a time when games at the top level, as depicted on television or reported in the press, are becoming a continuous series of rows, involving bad manners, bad temper and bad sportsmanship, and when there are inevitably signs of this type of behaviour spreading to a wider circle. But if, as I believe, we have not lowered our standards in these respects, we have at the same time fully maintained our standard of cricket and in doing so we have been helped by one important change. Fifty years ago a great preponderance of our members came from a very small range of public schools or from the services. Now the net is cast far wider, to the great benefit of the club both on and off the

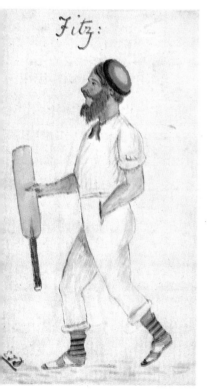

Top: H. W. Fellows (*left*) and A. N. Other (*right*), Badminton, 1862
Above right: Rev. E. T. Drake, 1862
Above centre: Unknown Zingaro, 20 June 1846
Above left: R. A. FitzGerald, 1861

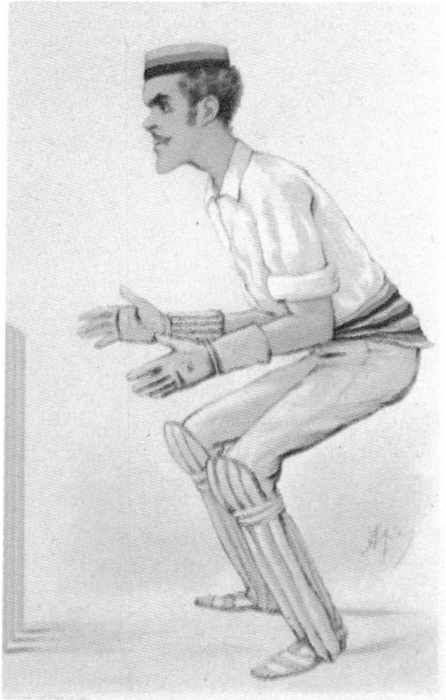

Top left: Founders – Sir Spencer Ponsonby Fane, J. L. Baldwin, Lord Bessborough

Above left: Hon. Alfred Lyttelton

Above centre: Capt. E. G. Wynyard

Above right: Lord Hawke

Top right: St Cross

Right: 21 June 1981. IZ *v.* Lavinia, Duchess of Norfolk's XI, Arundel Castle, (*left to right standing*) P. S. B. Rudd, N. E. Goodeve Docker, P. M. Davy, R. A. Hutton, C. J. T. Holland, C. F. Worlidge. (*Sitting*) Sir Ian Collett, Bt, G. P. S. Delisle, M. F. M. Wright (capt.), Commander M. P. Gretton, RN, D. A. Oldridge

Top: (*Left to right*) R. Leigh Pemberton, P. G. Lowndes, Mrs Leigh Pemberton, C. J. H. Green, Sir Mervyn Dunnington Jefferson, Bt
Above: R. Aird, Lord Home, Lavinia, Duchess of Norfolk

field. There must have been something wrong when such a fine cricketer as Harry Altham and a man so loved and respected could say that it had never occurred to him that he would ever be elected to IZ. As it was, he was thirty-five before this happened. No one whose memories go back to the 1920s or 1930s can doubt that the average IZ side is stronger now than in those days, as good in batting, better in bowling and infinitely more active in the field. In fact one is probably justified in saying that the club is now in a healthier condition than at any time since the Great War, and few now can remember farther back than that. Floruit, floret, florebit.

R. L. ARROWSMITH

8

IZ in First-Class Cricket

In 1851 and again in 1855 and 1862 IZ played Cambridge University. In that period it is often difficult to determine whether a match was first-class. There can be no doubt that these were not. There is no evidence that a third day had been allotted to any of them, the Cambridge sides were weakened because any members who were Zingari were claimed by IZ, and the IZ sides were no stronger than those which normally represented them in club cricket. In 1855 only five members appeared, the side being completed by undergraduates. In 1862 three of the best Cambridge cricketers, the Hon. C. G. Lyttelton, the Hon. T. de Grey and R. Lang, all of whom were in the Gentlemen's side that year or the next, assisted IZ. Lyttelton made 39 and 46, de Grey 18 in each innings, and Lang, a great fast bowler, made 45 and took the first three wickets. Even so, Cambridge won by an innings and 117 runs, which does not say much for the strength of the visitors.

For a match unquestionably first-class we have to wait till 1866. At this time and for many years after such was the importance of Canterbury Week that every effort was made to provide continuous cricket and, whenever one of the scheduled matches ended early, another game was immediately started, in which one side was frequently IZ. These games were not of course first-class. But in 1866 the second match of the week, 8, 9 and 10 August, was definitely announced as IZ *v.* the Gentlemen of the South.

The scores were Gentlemen of the South 97 (W. G. Grace 30, Capt. W. H. Parnell 5 for 42) and 226 (W. G. Grace 50, M. A. Troughton 40 not out); IZ 78 (R. Lipscomb 7 for 35) and 124 (W. F. Maitland 36, W. G. Grace 6 for 35, E. M. Grace 5 for 72). IZ lost by 121 runs.

At this time the North seldom had an amateur of any standing so that the Gentlemen of the South should have had approximately the same side as the Gentlemen at Lord's, less their IZ players. In fact, only E. M. and W. G. Grace had played for them at Lord's, though Lipscomb, the Kent fast bowler, did so two years later. Most of the others were only marginally of county standard. It will be seen how much the side owed to the Graces, especially as E.M. caught five catches. The match was twelve-a-side. Of the IZ side Alfred Lubbock and C. F. Buller, two of the best bats of the day, and W. F. Maitland, a fine all-rounder, had been in the side at Lord's, the Rev. J. McCormick would certainly have been had he been available and H. Arkwright, the best amateur slow bowler at this time, had played in 1862 and 1864. Two months later he was killed climbing Mont Blanc; his body, in a state of perfect preservation, was recovered in October 1897. Captain W. H. Parnell, a Rugbeian and a Guardsman, was a very fast bowler.

Between 1877 and 1890 IZ played every year but one in the Scarborough Festival.

1877, 27, 28, 29 August. IZ 103 and 93; Yorkshire 88 (R. G. Henderson 6 for 33) and 37 (Henderson 7 for 12). IZ won by 71 runs.

This was a fine performance as with the exception of Tom Armitage, a useful all-rounder, Yorkshire were at full strength. They included five players who, had it been necessary to pick an England eleven that year, would have been strong candidates, and another, Andrew Greenwood, who in fact had played in the very unrepresentative sides in the first two Tests the winter before. The five were George Ullyett, a great all-rounder, the two fast bowlers Tom Emmett and Allen Hill, George Pinder the wicketkeeper, and Ephraim Lockwood. If we had not the testimony of his contemporaries and of his scores to show what a good bat Lockwood was, we have his own statement: of his innings of 208 against Kent at Gravesend in 1883 he said, 'It was the finest innings I ever saw in my life.' R. G. Henderson, who won the match for IZ, was a slow-medium right-hander, who had not been in the eleven at Harrow, but took many wickets for Middlesex.

1878, 2, 3, 4 September. IZ 175 (A. J. Webbe 100) and 155 (A. J. Webbe 28); Yorkshire 296 (Ephraim Lockwood 61, R. G. Henderson 6 for 104) and 35 for 1 wicket. IZ lost by nine wickets.

Yorkshire were again at full strength. A. J. Webbe, for many years captain of Middlesex, was always a specially formidable batsman on a bad wicket or at a crisis.

1879, 4 5, 6 September. Yorkshire 298 (M. Riley 92, H. E. Rhodes 64, A. G. Steel 5 wickets) and 16 for 1; IZ 127 (H. R. Webbe 34 not out) and 341 (A. H. Evans 55, W. F. Forbes 53, W. H. Hadow 48). Drawn.

This match is not given in *Wisden* or *Lillywhite* and the IZ album does not give the bowling analysis. For Yorkshire Peate, the famous slow left-hander, took five wickets in each innings. On this occasion the Yorkshire side was far from representative. H. E. Rhodes was better known as an oar and ex-President of the Cambridge boat.

A. G. Steel, then in his second year at Cambridge, was for years a tower of strength, when he could find the time to play, for England, Lancashire and IZ. A. H. Evans was a notable Oxford fast bowler, but his action was so suspect that Lord Harris once refused to play for the Gentlemen at Lord's because he had been picked; he was father of A. J. Evans. H. R. Webbe, who died very young, was younger brother of A. J. Webbe, and like him captain of Oxford. W. H. Hadow was a fine Oxford and Middlesex batsman and a good change bowler.

W. F. Forbes, as he never went to the university or played for a county, is in danger of being forgotten. He was a beautiful attacking batsman, a bowler so fast that he sometimes had two long-stops and a magnificent field, who at Eton had thrown 132 yards measured. By all accounts his throwing was not confined to his fielding. Once when he was bowling for IZ, the batsman complained to the umpire, Martingell, who had coached Forbes at Eton, about it. All Martingell said was, 'Now, Mr Forbes, bowl a bit, bowl a bit.'

1880, 2, 3, 4 September. Yorkshire 168 (Ephraim Lockwood 69, H. E. Rhodes 49, A. G. Steel 6 for 52) and 76 (C. T. Studd 5 for 31, A. G. Steel 4 for 45); IZ 127 (A. G. Steel 45) and 118 for 7 (H. Whitfeld 79 not out). IZ won by three wickets.

This was a fine win over a strong side. C. T. Studd, then a freshman at Cambridge, had a very brief career in first-class cricket but was a great player, an extremely sound bat, who made two centuries against the great Australian side of 1882, a slow medium off-spinner with the accuracy of a professional, and a good field. At this time only W.G. had ever performed the double. C. T. Studd performed it twice while still an undergraduate, in 1882 and 1883. Only one undergraduate has done so since, G. L. Jessop in 1897.

Herbert Whitfeld, a Cambridge blue and a soccer international, later captained Sussex.

1881, 6, 7, 8 September. IZ 124 (Hon. A. Lyttelton 35, Hon. E. Lyttelton 34, Peate 6 for 63) and 236 (H. Whitfeld 63, W. F. Forbes 48, Hon. E. Lyttelton 46, Emmett 7 for 68); Yorkshire 121 (C. T. Studd 6 for 31) and 80 (Hon. M. B. Hawke 32, C. T. Studd 6 for 43). IZ won by 159 runs.

Another fine win. Lord Hawke, as he later became, was not yet a member. Edward Lyttelton, later headmaster of Eton, was a very good bat and had captained the great Cambridge side of 1878: he was now a schoolmaster and so was not in first-class practice. His younger brother, Alfred, was one of the great wicketkeepers and batsmen of his day. He was a soccer international, had also represented Cambridge at athletics, rackets and tennis and was for years the finest amateur tennis player in England. It was to his batting that the phrase 'the champagne of cricket' is said to have been first applied. He had later a distinguished career at the Bar and in politics.

1882, 4, 5, 6 September. Yorkshire 407 (Ephraim Lockwood 104 not out, Bates 76, H. E. Rhodes 63); IZ 126 (G. B. Studd 43, C. T. Studd 30, Peate 5 for 46) and 190 (Hon. E. Lyttelton 56, Hon. A. Lyttelton 40, Peate 5 for 75, Emmett 5 for 58). IZ lost by an innings and 91 runs.

IZ sadly missed A. G. Steel, probably at this time the second best all-rounder in England. G. B. Studd was a more attractive bat than his younger brother, C.T., but less sound; he was also a superbground-field at cover, though a slightly uncertain catcher. Both brothers went with the Hon. Ivo Bligh's team to Australia to recover the Ashes in the following winter.

1882 7, 8, 9 September *v.* the Australians, Drawn.

THE AUSTRALIANS

A. C. Bannerman	c A. Lyttelton b Forbes	8	not out	120
H. H. Massie	b Forbes	51	c and b Forbes	18
W. L. Murdoch	b Forbes	0	b Evans	53
P. S. McDonnell	b Forbes	0	b Evans	42
T. Horan	c Forbes b C. T. Studd	32	c A. Lyttelton b C. T. Studd	26
G. Giffen	c C. T. Studd b Forbes	3	c Lucas b C. T. Studd	15
G. J. Bonnor	c Lucas b Steel	17	not out	122
J. McC. Blackham	c Marriott b Forbes	15		
T. W. Garrett	c Steel b C. T. Studd	1		
H. F. Boyle	run out	12		
F. R. Spofforth	not out	9	b Steel	5
	Byes 3, leg byes 2	5	Byes 17, leg byes 5	22
		153		423

	O	M	R	W	O	M	R	W
C. T. Studd	17	10	23	2	36	18	61	2
A. H. Evans	14	7	18	0	27	8	80	2
W. F. Forbes	31.3	17	32	6	47	24	60	1
A. G. Steel	37	14	71	1	52	21	96	1
A. P. Lucas	4	1	4	0	3	1	27	1
Hon. A. Lyttelton					16	7	29	0
Lord Harris					13	3	28	0
Hon. E. Lyttelton					8	2	20	0

I ZINGARI

Hon. A. Lyttelton	c Blackham b Spofforth	6
G. B. Studd	c Bannerman b Boyle	86
A. P. Lucas	b Spofforth	26
C. T. Studd	c Bonnor b Boyle	21
Lord Harris	c Garrett b Spofforth	47
A. G. Steel	c Murdoch b Boyle	29
Hon. E. Lyttelton	b Spofforth	3
R. A. H. Mitchell	c sub. b Boyle	32
C. Marriott	c Garrett b Boyle	4
W. F. Forbes	c sub. b Boyle	0
A. H. Evans	not out	11
	Byes 9, leg byes 4, no-ball 1	14
		279

	O	M	R	W
F. R. Spofforth	69	30	106	4
G. Giffen	21	6	45	0
T. W. Garrett	15	6	17	0
H. F. Boyle	68.5	32	97	6

This was a notable performance, especially as for many years this Australian side was rated as the strongest they had sent over. It was of course the side which ten days before had defeated England at the Oval. Four of the IZ side had played in that match – Alfred Lyttelton, A. P. Lucas, A. G. Steel and C. T. Studd. Lord Harris had already played for England and G. B. Studd did so the following winter. All except Marriott, an Oxford Blue and a great stalwart of Leicestershire cricket, had played for the Gentlemen at Lord's. In the Australians' second innings Bannerman batted six and three-quarter hours for his 120 and Bonnor an hour and three-quarters for his 122; together they put on 167.

1883. IZ did not appear at Scarborough.

1884, 4, 5, 6 September *v.* The Australians. IZ lost by eight wickets.

I ZINGARI

H. Whitfeld	b Spofforth	1	b Spofforth	6
W. H. Patterson	b Spofforth	10	b Palmer	26
Lord Harris	b Spofforth	24	c Scott b Spofforth	3
A. G. Steel	c McDonnell b Spofforth	15	c Boyle b Midwinter	20
Hon. A. Lyttelton	c McDonnell b Spofforth	37	run out	1
G. B. Studd	b Spofforth	3	b Spofforth	28
W. F. Forbes	st Blackham b Midwinter	80	b Spofforth	10
W. H. Hadow	b Bonnor	25	c Blackham b Spofforth	7
P. J. de Paravicini	b Spofforth	3	not out	15
C. E. Cottrell	b Midwinter	15	b Spofforth	0
S. Christopherson	not out	0	c Scott b Spofforth	14
Byes 5, leg byes 7, wides 4		16	Byes 5, leg byes 3, no-balls 2	10
		229		140

	O	M	R	W	O	M	R	W
F. R. Spofforth	57	22	114	7	42.2	22	71	7
H. F. Boyle	30	14	47	0				
G. E. Palmer	11	4	17	0	15	4	30	1
W. Midwinter	6.2	2	10	2	33	21	29	
G. Giffen	3	0	13	0	1	1	0	0
G. J. Bonnor	4	1	12	1				

THE AUSTRALIANS

P. S. McDonnell	c Patterson b Cottrell	20	c Christopherson b Steel	67
A. C. Bannerman	b Steel	10	c Lyttelton b Forbes	10
W. L. Murdoch	b Cottrell	14	not out	36
H. J. H. Scott	b Cottrell	7	not out	15
G. Giffen	c Christopherson b Cottrell	34		
G. J. Bonnor	c and b Steel	21		
J. McC. Blackham	b Steel	8		
W. Midwinter	not out	49		
G. E. Palmer	c Forbes b Steel	4		
F. R. Spofforth	c Whitfeld b Steel	49		
H. F. Boyle	c Steel b Cottrell	2		
	Byes 9, leg byes 6	15	Byes 7, leg byes 2, wide 1, no-ball 1	11
		233		139

	O	M	R	W	O	M	R	W
C. E. Cottrell	41	20	72	5	16	4	46	0
W. F. Forbes	32	17	28	0	6	4	13	1
S. Christopherson	9	3	22	0	6	3	9	0
A. G. Steel	37	13	76	5	13	4	35	1
Hon. A. Lyttelton	3	0	8	0	2	0	8	0
W. H. Hadow	3	1	12	0				
H. Whitfeld					5	1	17	0

This Australian side was regarded as a strong one, though not quite the equal of its predecessor, and IZ had no reason to feel dissatisfied. Indeed when they had eight of their opponents out for 140, they must even have had visions of victory, but then Midwinter and Spofforth put on 91. They had no reason to be ashamed of being bowled out by Spofforth, then at his peak and widely regarded as the greatest bowler that had yet appeared. Four of the IZ side, Lord Harris, Steel, Lyttelton and Christopherson, a fast bowler, had played for England that year. C. T. Studd had retired earlier in the summer from serious cricket to become a missionary. C. E. Cottrell was a medium-pace bowler who did useful work for Middlesex, and in club cricket was also a heavy scorer.

From this time IZ were less ambitious at Scarborough and contented themselves with playing sides entitled 'The Gentlemen of England', which though not representative of the full strength of the Gentlemen, were usually reasonably strong.

1885, 31 August, 1, 2 September. IZ 374 (J. G. Walker 111, A. J.

Webbe 82 retired hurt) and 132 for 2 (G. B. Studd 59 not out, Hon. A. Lyttelton 47 not out); Gentlemen 298 (H. W. Bainbridge 76, W. G. Grace 63, A. G. Steel 5 for 102, G. H. Portal 4 for 55). Drawn.

J. G. Walker, no relation of the Walkers of Southgate, failed to get a Blue at Oxford, but made many runs for Middlesex and represented the Gentlemen at Lord's. G. H. Portal, a fast left-hander, had been a good all-rounder at Eton, but a distinguished career abroad in the diplomatic service gave him little chance of playing later. He was only thirty-five when he died, having already been knighted. H. W. Bainbridge, for many years Captain of Warwickshire, was later a member.

1886, 30, 31 August, 1 September. Gentlemen 90 (A. G. Steel 7 for 61) and 266 (C. I. Thornton 107 not out, A. E. Stoddart 57); IZ 299 (Cecil Wilson 86, G. B. Studd 55, W. E. W. Collins 5 for 108) and 58 for 2. IZ won by eight wickets.

Cecil Wilson, later Bishop of Bunbury, did not get a Blue at Cambridge, but made many runs for Kent, when they could get him. W. E. W. Collins, another who failed to get a Blue, in his case at Oxford, was a prominent Free Forester who met with astonishing success in the few first-class matches he played in: he never played for a county. A fast left-hander, he was a terror in club cricket, and once removed four batsmen with one ball. He split the thumb of number eight, who had to retire; number nine at the other end fainted at the sight of the blood. Number ten said he 'had liefer take part in a prize fight than face such a bowler and refused to go in' so there was no one to bat with number eleven. In 1874 he made 338 not out in Freshwater on a ground where there were no boundaries and in 1886, going in last against the Australians at Scarborough, scored 56 not out, allegedly scoring from every ball he received. What a man! In his will he founded the Free Forester Scholarships at Oxford.

But the chief feature of this match was C. I. Thornton's innings. His 107 took only seventy minutes and included eight sixes, a six in those days meaning a hit clean out of the ground. Having hit two consecutive balls through the same window of a house in Trafalgar Square, he sensibly suggested that the window should be left open. A lady, hearing this story, asked whether the match had been at Lord's or the Oval.

1887, 29, 30, 31 August. Gentlemen 381 (C. I. Thornton 107, A. E. Stoddart 116, W. G. Grace 73) and 32 for no wicket; IZ 264 (A. J. Webbe 76, H. W. Forster 37, Prince Christian Victor 35,

W. E. W. Collins 5 for 76) and 308 (A. J. Webbe 126, Hon. A. Lyttelton 50, Hon. M. B. Hawke 47). Drawn.

The IZ bowling was perhaps the weakest ever seen in a first-class match. Only H. W. Forster, later Lord Forster, a slow left-hander and an Oxford Blue, who played for Hampshire, had really any claims to be more than an occasional change. Alfred Lyttelton's 50 was his last innings in first-class cricket. This was Prince Christian Victor's only appearance in first-class cricket, though he was a heavy scorer in army and club cricket and probably the second best wicketkeeper at Oxford in his time. C. I. Thornton's 107, again made in seventy minutes, included on this occasion only three sixes. These two innings must have given him particular pleasure as he is said always to have been sore at not being a member of IZ.

1888, 30, 31, August. IZ 135 (A. J. Webbe 39 not out, E. M. Hadow 34, F. R. Spofforth 7 for 67) and 171 (A. J. Webbe 75, E. M. Hadow 31, F. G. J. Ford 5 for 51, F. R. Spofforth 4 for 57); Gentlemen 99 (W. C. Hedley 6 for 49) and 98 (H. W. Forster 7 for 37). IZ won by 109 runs.

E. M. Hadow, a brother of W. H. and a good attacking bat, played for Middlesex. W. C. Hedley was a fast bowler with an action so doubtful that Lord Harris refused to have him in the Kent side. He played for years for Somerset and represented the Gentlemen, but was put on the blacklist in 1900 by the county captains, determined to eradicate throwing. Spofforth had just come to live in England.

1889 29, 30 August. IZ 102 (S. M. J. Woods 4 for 38) and 165 (A. G. Steel 65, S. M. J. Woods 7 for 62); Gentlemen 203 (W. G. Grace 58) and 66 for 5. IZ lost by five wickets.

1890, 28, 29, 30 August. Gentlemen 85 (W. C. Hedley 6 for 36) and 219 (H. T. Hewett 99, H. J. Mordaunt 5 for 17); IZ 104 (S. M. J. Woods 7 for 47) and 107 (A. J. Webbe 43, S. M. J. Woods 5 for 50, W. G. Grace 4 for 18). IZ lost by 93 runs.

There was no disgrace in being bowled out for the second year running by Sam Woods, at this time the finest fast bowler in the world. Years later Sir Pelham Warner described him as 'the most artistic of all fast bowlers'. He had a wonderfully disguised slow ball. H. T. Hewett, Captain of Somerset and later a Zingaro himself, was a great left-handed hitter, especially on a bad wicket. H. J. Mordaunt, a member of a notable IZ family, is best remembered for his hundred for Cambridge in the Varsity match. At Eton he had originally been a pretty successful fast-medium bowler, but in his last year he moderated his pace and headed the averages.

This was IZ's last appearance in the Scarborough Festival. After this they played twice only in first-class cricket, in 1895 and in 1904, both times against the Gentlemen of England at Lord's. The 1895 match was arranged specially to mark the club's fiftieth anniversary, and the two surviving founders, Sir Spencer Ponsonby-Fane and J. L. Baldwin, were photographed with the team. For fear that IZ might not be able to raise a strong enough side, A. E. Stoddart, then one of the best batsmen in England, was specially made a member and this had much to do with the decision not to attempt first-class cricket in future. It was felt, rightly, that however suitable Stoddart himself was for membership, it was a dangerous precedent.

1895, 20, 21, 22 June *v.* Gentlemen of England at Lord's.

I ZINGARI

H. T. Hewett	st MacGregor b Grace sen.	51	b Fry	22
F. S. Jackson	c Grace jun. b Fry	34	c Grace sen. b Grace jun.	23
A. E. Stoddart	c MacGregor b Fry	38	c Hill b Massie	92
G. J. Mordaunt	b Fry	19	b Massie	42
Capt. E. G. Wynyard	c Hill b Grace jun.	56	c and b Fry	51
Sir T. C. O'Brien	c Hill b Fry	20	c Grace sen. b Hill	5
G. F. Vernon	b Fry	0	c MacGregor b Hill	17
A. G. Steel	not out	38	l.b.w. b Fry	14
L. C. V. Bathurst	b Burnup	4	b Fry	6
H. Philipson	b Burnup	15	not out	8
H. R. Bromley-Davenport	c and b Burnup	1	c MacGregor b Fry	0
	Byes 7, leg byes 4, wide 1 no-ball 1	13	Byes 8, leg bye 1, wides 4	13
		289		293

	O	M	R	W	O	M	R	W
C. J. Burnup	23.4	5	82	3	12	5	34	0
W. G. Grace jun.	12	2	40	1	11	3	30	1
C. B. Fry	27	6	75	5	26.4	2	102	5
W. G. Grace sen.	16	0	79	1	5	1	20	0
H. H. Massie					14	2	39	2
V. T. Hill					22	8	55	2

GENTLEMEN OF ENGLAND

W. G. Grace sen.	b Steel	34	not out	101
A. Sellers	c Philipson b Davenport	10	not out	70
R. S. Lucas	c Mordaunt b Steel	18		
R. W. Rice	l.b.w. b Bathurst	1		
C. B. Fry	b Jackson	43		
H. H. Massie	c Vernon b Jackson	26		
W. G. Grace jun.	c Stoddart b Steel	79		
V. T. Hill	c Mordaunt b Davenport	73		
C. J. Burnup	not out	66		
G. MacGregor	c Hewett b Davenport	21		
A. T. Kemble	b Bathurst	30		
	Byes 4, leg byes 2, wides 3, no ball 1	10	Wide 1	1
		411		172

	O	M	R	W	O	M	R	W
F. S. Jackson	39	16	96	2	15	6	40	0
H. R. Bromley-Davenport	35	7	100	3	6	0	32	0
A. G. Steel	28	0	92	3	7	1	17	0
L. V. C. Bathurst	21.2	4	53	2	11	0	46	0
A. E. Stoddart	15	4	38	0	8.1	2	36	0
Capt. E. G. Wynyard	5	2	22	0				

IZ lost by ten wickets. They had a strong batting side, the only important absentee being A. C. MacLaren, who at that moment had a job at a prep. school. Their bowling was probably the best they could have produced, apart from W. C. Hedley, who that year headed the first-class averages; their wicketkeeper, Hylton Philipson, had kept in four of the five Tests in Australia in the previous winter. But the Gentlemen were far from representative. Only three of them, W.G., Fry and MacGregor, had ever played for them at Lord's, though Burnup, whose first first-class match this was, did so later. Their bowling was desperately weak. Young W.G.'s four wickets for Cambridge that year cost 73 runs each, his father's record for the season was 16 wickets at 32 runs each, and Burnup, who afterwards made so many runs for Cambridge and Kent, was never more than an occasional change, though he did once bowl out the Australians at Canterbury. Fry was at this time regarded as an all-rounder: he was fast but, as far as one can gather, was looked on by everyone except himself as a thrower not a bowler. His bowling career ended in 1898 when he was no-balled by three of the leading umpires. Further evidence of the difficulty the Gentlemen experienced in raising their side is that they included two wicketkeepers, MacGregor and

Kemble, neither of whom was worth a place purely as a bat. However, despite all this, they won easily enough in the end, W.G. and Arthur Sellers, father of Brian Sellers, hitting off the runs in 105 minutes. It will be seen therefore that IZ were bowling their overs (five-ball overs in those days) at more than twenty-six an hour. H. H. Massie, the famous Australian hitter, was on holiday in England at the time. This was A. G. Steel's last appearance in a first-class match.

In March 1904 the surviving founder, Sir Spencer Ponsonby-Fane, reached his eightieth birthday and in honour of this IZ entertained him at dinner on 6 June at the Prince's Restaurant, Piccadilly. No doubt it was also to mark this occasion that they went back on their decision not to play first-class cricket and arranged a match against the Gentlemen of England at Lord's to coincide with the dinner.

6, 7, 8 June 1904, *v.* the Gentlemen of England.

GENTLEMEN

J. E. Raphael	b Bosanquet	8	l.b.w. b Hartley	33
L. J. Moon	c Mordaunt b Cunliffe	162	b Steel	39
G. W. Beldam	c Newton b Mordaunt	18	b Bosanquet	36
H. H. Marriott	st Newton b Bosanquet	3	b Bosanquet	11
R. W. Nicholls	l.b.w. b Bosanquet	7	st Newton b Mordaunt	0
H. F. Montgomery	b Bosanquet	2	b Heseltine	39
J. A. Berners	c Wynyard b Bosanquet	4	c Lucas b Bosanquet	50
C. J. Kortright	b Bosanquet	7	c Hartley b Heseltine	3
K. J. Key	not out	38	c Heseltine b Steel	52
H. Hesketh Prichard	b Cunliffe	2	not out	5
C. Headlam	b Bosanquet	4	l.b.w. b Bosanquet	11
Byes 9, leg bye 1, no-balls 2		12	Byes 30, leg byes 4, wides 4, no balls 2	40
		267		319

	O	M	R	W		O	M	R	W
B. J. T. Bosanquet	25.3	2	83	7		21.2	4	68	4
C. Heseltine	6	1	30	0		10	1	28	2
E. C. Mordaunt	20	6	40	1		8	1	34	1
F. H. E. Cunliffe	16	2	58	2		8	0	38	0
A. J. L. Hill	2	0	28	0					
E. E. Steel	7	1	16	0		17	4	63	2
					J. C. Hartley	16	4	48	1

I ZINGARI

Capt. E. G. Wynyard	c Moon b Montgomery	45	b Key	147
A. P. Lucas	c Marriott b Prichard	4	b Prichard	20
A. J. L. Hill	b Prichard	0	l.b.w. b Montgomery	38
B. J. T. Bosanquet	b Prichard	4	not out	66
Lord Hawke	b Kortright	43	not out	6
F. H. E. Cunliffe	b Prichard	11		
E. E. Steel	b Prichard	11	c Raphael b Prichard	111
E. C. Mordaunt	b Kortright	5		
J. C. Hartley	not out	15		
A. E. Newton	b Kortright	13		
C. Heseltine	absent	0		
Byes 16, leg byes 6, wide 1		23	Byes 16, leg byes 7, no-ball 1	24
		175		412

	O	M	R	W		O	M	R	W
H. Hesketh Prichard	18	4	65	5		31	3	112	2
G. W. Beldam	9	0	36	0		12	0	53	0
C. J. Kortright	13.2	5	36	3		23	2	90	0
H. F. Montgomery	4	0	15	1		19	0	74	1
					J. E. Raphael	6	0	34	0
					K. J. Key	2.2	0	9	1
					L. J. Moon	2	0	16	0

IZ won by six wickets. In the absence of F. S. Jackson, A. C. MacLaren, J. R. Mason, F. L. Fane and the brothers H. K. and R. E. Foster, they were far below full strength: with these to help them they might well have tested a fully representative side of the Gentlemen. As it was, their batting was fair, but their only bowler of any standing was Bosanquet, then in his brief prime as a googly bowler, and, as their average age was thirty-six or so, they can hardly have been brilliant in the field. But the Gentlemen's side, in a great era of amateur cricket, was hopelessly misnamed. Hesketh Prichard, a fast bowler and a man of many parts, well known as a traveller and author and an expert sniper in the Great War, was the only one who played for the Gentlemen at Lord's this year, though Beldam did so in 1905: none of the others can have been in the running. Kortright's great days as a fast bowler were long past and Key had retired from regular first-class cricket in 1899. Even so it will be seen that up to a point they made a good match of it, but on the last day Wynyard and Steel put on 201 for the second wicket. Steel, a younger brother of A.G. and like him a leg-spinner and a good batsman, returning to

England after many years abroad, had for a year or two been a considerable help to Lancashire. *Wisden* says that Wynyard 'was batting over three-and-a-half hours and scarcely made a mistake'. In fact he was so dissatisfied with his own form in the morning that, summoning the three best pro bowlers available, he kept them bowling at him through the luncheon interval and, when play restarted, he emerged from the practice ground to join his partner at the wicket.

Since 1904 IZ have not attempted a first-class match.

R. L. ARROWSMITH

9
Some Notable Zingari – I

THE Hon. Frederick Ponsonby, who succeeded as Earl of Bessborough in 1880, will always have a place in cricket history on two accounts; he was one of the founders of IZ and he and his inseparable friend, the Hon. Robert Grimston, were for years the powers behind Harrow cricket. Day after day in the summer from about 1845 on they would go down to the school from London, often walking both ways, to coach, help and advise the boys. Further, they made themselves responsible for keeping the school supplied with competent pros, and for these Ponsonby normally paid himself. Such intervention by old boys can easily become tiresome and it is a great tribute to the tact and charm of the pair that they are never mentioned save with gratitude and affection. There was, of course, in those days no such thing as a master appointed to run the cricket and it was a pure accident whether there was anyone on the staff who knew anything about the game. Fred Ponsonby never volunteered suggestions or interfered; he never captained the side from the boundary, as R. A. H. Mitchell did for Eton, and, indeed, as Robert Grimston had done for Harrow, until he was requested not to. He made it clear that he was there to help and advise if asked nor did he complain if his advice was not taken. As one Harrow Captain wrote later, 'There never was, or will be, anyone who could teach cricket as he could.' He had himself been in the Harrow and Cambridge elevens and had played for the Gentlemen from 1836 to 1845, after which trouble with an arm made him confine himself to less important cricket, which he continued to play for some years. In an age when batsmen were divided into forward players, like Pilch, or back players, like Wenman, he used to play in 'a fine free forward style, hitting well', but was also a good cutter and 'an excellent judge of the short run'. He was too a fine field. The Ponsonbys were nephews of Lord Frederick Beauclerk, the greatest cricketer of his day and one of the most remarkable, if not the most estimable, characters in cricket history. Both brothers played occasionally for Surrey.

The younger, later Sir Spencer Ponsonby-Fane and our first Governor, was also a good player, 'a free and lively hitter, forward and to leg' and a good field. Moreover, he was very fast between the wickets, but an uncertain judge of a run, responsible for many run-outs. Apart from all that he did for IZ, he was a great figure at Lord's. Elected in 1840, he had in fact played for MCC in 1839 at the age of fifteen: the side had included Benjamin Aislabie, who was born in 1774. He was Treasurer of MCC from 1879 and a Trustee from 1900, holding both offices till his death, and he several times refused the Presidency. He also laid the foundation of the unique collection of cricket pictures, books and relics of all kinds in the pavilion. He had, besides, a distinguished public career: among the positions he held was Comptroller of the Lord Chamberlain's office and Bath King of Arms. His home for the last forty years of his life was Brympton d'Evercy, near Yeovil, which is now cared for by Charles Clive-Ponsonby-Fane, himself a Zingaro, who has set up in it a small IZ museum. When Sir Spencer died in 1915, he was a link with an incredibly distant past.

Our third Founder, John Loraine Baldwin, was never a prominent cricketer, nor was our Perpetual President, William Bolland, but both were keen and both took their share of wickets in the early days of the club. On the other hand R. P. Long, 'who under mesmeric influence assisted at the séance' at which IZ was founded and is believed to have suggested our name in a lucid interval, was, during a brief career, a distinctly good batsman. He had been in the Harrow XI and played for Cambridge in 1845 and 1846. In 1845 in the first innings he made the top score, 36 out of a total of 112. Next year in the second innings he was again top scorer with 39 not out. Playing a few weeks later for the Gentlemen, he had much to do with their victory by one wicket, being top scorer with 34 in a total of 105 in the first innings and in the second carrying out his bat for 9 at the crisis. This was the end of his first-class career: indeed, he seems to have played little cricket of any kind even for IZ, of which he was the first Secretary. Later generations of the family have contributed several members to the club and particularly his son, the first Lord Long of Wraxall, who was for many years on the Biennial Committee.

Unquestionably the most distinguished cricketer among the original members was C. G. Taylor, one of the best bats in England and generally reckoned the most attractive: no one had so wide a range of strokes. An Etonian and a Cambridge Blue, he played for Sussex and represented the Gentlemen from 1836 to 1846, when for some unexplained reason he gave up regular cricket. He continued to play occasionally and at long intervals until the end of the fifties, even reappearing in some first-class matches in 1853 and 1854. Doubtless his most famous innings was 89 for the Gentlemen against the Players in 1843, which had much to do with the Gentlemen winning by an innings and 20 runs. On this occasion he was out 'hat knocked on wicket b Hillyer': Fuller Pilch had been out in the same way batting for the Players in 1837. In each of the first two matches played by IZ Taylor made over 50. He was also an effective slow round-arm bowler and a superb off-side field. For years he was the best amateur tennis player in England: there was no amateur championship in those days, but he was reckoned to be about fifteen behind the professional champion, Edmund Tompkins. He was also a first-class billiards player. Nor was this the end of his accomplishments. He once bet a friend that he would make himself a pair of trousers and wear them on the King's Parade at Cambridge. 'He won his bet and nobody would have guessed that the things were not made by a professional person.' Another bet, which he also won, was that he would learn to play the piano and sing in less than six weeks. He was great-grandfather of Quentin Stanham, who has done so much for IZ Australia.

A few more of the original members deserve mention. The Hon. Robert Grimston, who in conjunction with Frederick Ponsonby later did so much for Harrow cricket, was the club's Treasurer and Auditor and played frequently for it. He gripped the bat with the back of both hands behind the handle and was primarily a solid player, but could hit hard in front of the wicket and was particularly effective against fast bowling. When opposed to Alfred Mynn, he always took in two bats, a heavy one for use against Mynn and one of the ordinary weight for the other bowlers. He appeared on several occasions for the Gentlemen. R. J. P. Broughton had played four years for Harrow, where he was head of the school as well as Captain of Cricket, and three for Cambridge, but could not spare much time for first-class cricket after he came down. However he played for years for IZ. He was a fine attacking batsman, credited with some very long hits, a wonderful cover and in his schooldays a formidable bowler. For forty-seven years up till his death in 1911 he was a Trustee of MCC.

The Rev. Cyril Randolph, an Oxford Blue, took a lot of wickets for the club in its first few years. An interesting figure is E. S. E. Hartopp, whose fame depended wholly on his long-stopping. He did not bowl and is described as an inferior bat (his highest score in an important match was 27), yet he was two years in the Cambridge side and played for the Gentlemen. When one learns that Wenman, the greatest wicketkeeper of the day, never attempted to take the ball (at any rate from a quick bowler) unless there was a chance of a catch or a stump, one can see the importance of the long-stop – and here Hartopp was unsurpassed. Indeed he was known as 'Mr Fellows's long-stop'. Harvey Fellows, who took many wickets for IZ, occupied for three years, 1847 to 1850, the same position among bowlers as Kortright did fifty years later – hardly anyone who played him reckoned he had ever faced a faster bowler. We have the authority of Lord Harris, who cannot have played with him until he was years past his best, that when long-stopping to him he heard the ball hum and one can easily understand that, without someone like Hartopp to save the byes, they could have reached astronomical proportions.

William Ward, elected in 1846, deserves a place here not only as a notable cricketer but as a link with an incredibly remote past. He had first played at Lord's in 1810, but, as he was then twenty-three, must have been playing for some years before that. Indeed he is said to have played for Hampshire in 1801 at the age of fourteen; if so, the score has been lost. He is also said to have used the same bat for fifty years but granted that bats had in those days far greater lasting powers than the modern ones and that he was certainly an expert at middling the ball, the story cannot hold water. Ward stood six foot one and played his last match when he was sixty; no boy of ten could possibly wield a bat suited to a man of that size, nor, if he had tried to do so, could he ever have become a good player. Moreover the bat in question weighed four pounds. Doubtless it was the weapon with which he made the first century ever scored for the Gentlemen against the Players and also his 278 for MCC against Norfolk in 1820, which was not only by more than a hundred runs the highest innings then recorded, but remained for fifty-six years the highest in an important match and, until Percy Holmes beat it in 1925, the highest at Lord's. For years he was one of the best, at times perhaps the best, batsmen in England. More important, when Thomas Lord, after whom Lord's is named, wished in 1825 to sell most of the ground for development, Ward saved the situation by buying Lord's interest for £5000. As he presided at the meeting in 1845 at which the

Surrey County Cricket Club was formed, he may be said to have been largely responsible for both Lord's and the Oval. It is a great tribute to the affection which he inspired in the young that he should have been elected to IZ when he was old enough to have been the father of almost any of the other members. What is more, he played several times for us and his last appearance on the cricket field was for IZ *v.* Bramshill in July 1847. In a match in which 247 runs were scored for thirty-four wickets, his contributions were 13 and 20 and in his last innings he was run out. A contemporary account stresses the beauty of his batting on this occasion.

Less eminent, but a great wicket-taker for IZ for a few years was C. J. Harenc, of whom William Lillywhite once said, 'I bowl the best ball in England and Mr Harenc the next.' This eulogy is not borne out by his record in first-class cricket. In fifteen matches for Kent four wickets stand in his name and in six matches for the Gentlemen, six. However it is probable that, as a slow bowler, he relied a good deal on catches and stumpings, for neither of which in those days was the bowler's name given. Anyhow Herbert Jenner, who constantly played with him for West Kent, actually regarded him as more difficult to play than Lillywhite, though far less accurate. Another successful slow bowler in IZ cricket at this period was Captain P. H. Mundy, a gunner, later a general, who had represented the Gentlemen in 1842 as a solid batsman. But the scores in club cricket in those days show that it was difficult to make runs, easy to take wickets. One who played much for the club at this time and was for years its Secretary and later its Chancellor, was the Hon. Sir Edward Chandos Leigh, an awkward but effective bat and a fine long-stop, who was three years in the Oxford XI. He was one of the founders of the Oxford Harlequins and was President of MCC in 1887, an especial honour as it was the centenary year and his felicitous speech at the dinner to commemorate this was long remembered. He was brother-in-law of R. A. FitzGerald, of whom more anon, and uncle of Sir Henry Leveson-Gower.

Two who played much IZ cricket for some years were the Hon. Cecil Fiennes, who took a fair number of wickets with fast underhands and for a time shared the duties of Secretary with Chandos Leigh, and his younger brother, Wingfield, a far better player, who had been three years in the Oxford side. He was a medium-pace round-arm bowler who once took five wickets in a club match with consecutive balls, and was very successful for IZ; he was also a good enough bat to score a hundred for the club in days when hundreds were rare. Another great acquisition was the Rev. E. T. Drake, elected in 1853 and a loyal supporter for many years. He had been three years in the Cambridge side and appeared eight times for the Gentlemen, for whom he played a notable innings in 1857. They went in to get 128 and were all out for 114, of which he scored 58. Only one other batsman reached double figures. He was a tremendous hitter who used a phenomenally heavy bat, a glorious field and as a lob bowler was reckoned at this time second only to V. E. Walker; he gave the ball air and turned it from leg. One could perhaps fairly classify him as a good player in first-class cricket and a great club player.

A less accomplished cricketer, but one who was at least as devoted to IZ, was R. A. FitzGerald. He had been three years in the Harrow side and played for Cambridge in 1854 and 1856; in 1855 he was not available to play at Lord's. As a batsman he believed in hitting the ball and made some historic hits, including one over the old tennis court (where the Mound Stand now is) into the St John's Wood Road. He was a magnificent fieldsman at long-leg and for IZ often did useful work as a fast round-arm bowler. He was a splendid match manager, much in demand, and constantly contributed to *Bell's Life* very witty reports of the matches in which he had played. Apart from these he helped considerably with the editing of several volumes of Haygarth's *Cricket Scores and Biographies* and made two major original contributions to cricket literature, *Wickets in the West*, an account of the amateur team he took to Canada in 1872 (which included W.G. and Lord Harris), and *Jerks in from Short Leg*, a series of humorous sketches. But above all he should be remembered as Secretary of MCC from 1864 to 1876, during which time the membership increased from 650 to 2080, 'a result mainly attributable to the zeal, ability and popularity of the Secretary'. He is indeed one of the most notable figures in the long history of Lord's.

At the beginning of the sixties IZ could, and sometimes did, produce a very strong side, as strong perhaps as those which twenty years later opposed Yorkshire or the Australians. Of the side for instance against the Free Foresters at Rugby in 1863 eight, the Rev. C. D. B. Marsham and his brother R. H. B., the Rev. E. T. Drake, the Rev. C. G. Lane, the Hon. C. G. Lyttelton, the Hon. Spencer Ponsonby, H. Arkwright and R. A. H. Mitchell, played for the Gentlemen about this time; most of them indeed were automatic selections as long as they could play. They included the two best amateur bowlers of the day, Arkwright, a slow right-hander, and

C. D. B. Marsham, very accurate fast-medium with a lot of life. These, with Drake's lobs, were a good start for a bowling side. Lyttelton, grandfather of our late Governor and the first of that great family to be a member, had ceased to bowl owing to an injury, but was a magnificent bat and a good wicketkeeper. Doubtless however the best batsman on the side was R. A. H. Mitchell, a notable Zingaro, not only because he played constantly for the club for many years, but because for some thirty years he trained all the leading Eton batsmen in a great era of Eton cricket and most of them later became members. He had captained Eton in 1861 and was asked to play for the Gentlemen that year; as it was in term-time, leave was naturally refused. His career for IZ began a few weeks after leaving and he played no fewer than fifteen innings for them that summer with considerable success. In his first match against the Staffordshire Hunt at Beaudesert, he had a curious experience. In the second innings he was given run out by 'Cocky' Royston, the IZ umpire, when he was well past the wicket. After the game, which IZ had won by 353 runs, Royston apologized. 'I say, Squire, I was obliged to give you out, because we couldn't have won the match in the time if you had stayed in. We're obliged to consider them things you know, else 'ow are we going to win our matches?' There were of course no declarations in those days. Mitchell captained Oxford for three years and represented the Gentlemen each year he was up, but then, becoming a schoolmaster and not being qualified for a first-class county, his first-class cricket was almost confined to Canterbury Week and later the Scarborough Festival, in which he appeared till 1883. In his prime he was undoubtedly one of the best (some would have said before the advent of W.G., *the* best) bats in England and such was the correctness of his style that no less a judge than the Rev. Edward Lyttelton has left it on record that he learnt more at Eton by simply watching Mitchell bat than by his actual instruction, fine coach though he undoubtedly was.

Two valuable recruits in the sixties were Alfred Lubbock and C. F. Buller. Both were beautiful stylists and a delight to watch. Lubbock, a great all-round athlete and a man of much charm, was a hard-working banker and could never spare much time for first-class cricket, but for years he was a certainty for the Gentlemen whenever they could get him and there was never any doubt of his right to be classed among the best bats of the day. Buller was a gentleman of leisure and for some years seems to have done little but play cricket. He was a regular member of the Middlesex side and in between played club cricket almost daily, much of it for IZ, for whom he scored heavily. Then he dropped out for a few seasons to reappear in 1874; but though he still got runs, he had grown very heavy and the magic had gone. Another great social figure who played constantly for IZ was W. G. Middleton, always known as 'Bay'. He was very deaf and an inveterate practical joker, but immensely popular and one of the finest amateur horsemen of his time. He was also a useful all-round cricketer who took many wickets for the club and was good enough to play in some of their first-class matches at Scarborough. He was killed riding in a point-to-point in 1892. Spencer Gore, a nephew of the brothers Ponsonby and Captain of Harrow in 1869, had actually been elected in 1867 and in 1868 had made a lot of runs for IZ in the holidays. Later he appeared occasionally for Surrey, but is best remembered as the first lawn-tennis champion at Wimbledon in 1877. The Rev. Osbert Mordaunt, the first Zingaro of a family that has supplied us with members ever since, had been in the Eton XI in 1860 as a hard-hitting bat, but gradually developed into a formidable lob bowler who took countless wickets for IZ and was prepared to bowl equally right or left-hand. An even better exponent of this art however was W. M. Rose. A wet-bob at Eton and handicapped by wearing spectacles, then sufficiently unusual on the cricket field to attract attention (there was no safety glass in those days), he appeared first for IZ as a useful opening batsman, but by practice turned himself into probably for a short time the best lob bowler in England. In the two matches of Canterbury Week in 1871 he took twenty-one wickets with an average of 8.5, and eleven of these were batsmen of a really high standard. In between he was struck 152 yards by C. I. Thornton. What he could do against less good players he showed on R. A. FitzGerald's tour in Canada in 1872, where he was credited with 136 wickets at a little over three runs each. It is interesting to notice the success which still attended lobs in good cricket forty years after round-arm bowling had been legalized and at a time indeed when all restriction on the height of the arm had been removed.

A notable election in 1871 was the Hon. George Harris, later Lord Harris, who for years ruled the cricket world with a rod of iron. Yet for all his other interests and commitments both in cricket and in other spheres, he always found time to take a full and active part in IZ. Like R. A. H. Mitchell, he played a lot for the club in August 1870, the year he left school, and he was still playing and making runs for it more than fifty years later. For years too he was a member of the Biennial Committee and rarely missed a meeting. Someone who went to visit him in his last illness found him sitting up in bed wearing an IZ blazer. No doubt in his later years people regarded playing under him as a frightening ordeal. I have a vivid recollection of his captaining BB against the Buffs at Canterbury and of four enormous skiers going up in quick succession off his lobs, a visibly trembling Brother circling under each. All were safely caught; he did not take kindly to those who dropped catches off him. As against this, I remember the first time I ever played with him, when he was captaining the East Kent Yeomanry and I was batting for BB. I played a ball to cover, who tossed it back to the bowler so carelessly that it fell several yards in front of him as he was strolling back to his mark. I beckoned with my finger to my partner and we had crossed in silence before the bowler realized what was happening. His Lordship came up to me and said, 'First young batsman I've seen in England this year who keeps his eyes open.' The praise from such a source to a young and indifferent cricketer was very sweet and I have never forgotten it. Of course I knew that had I backed up too eagerly when he was bowling or picked the ball up and returned it to the bowler, he would have had me out at once, for he played strictly to the laws. A splendid corrective to the idea which many who did not know him, and some who did, have of his character is provided by a photo in a recent book on Eton which shows him padded and waiting to take his innings on 4 June, when he was close on seventy: he is so obviously blissfully happy, watching with all the eagerness of a boy of fifteen, and the boys round him look happy too.

However, perhaps the most regular performer for IZ in the seventies was, suitably, J. H. Ponsonby, eldest son of Sir Spencer; the two constantly played together for the club. A member of the Harrow XI in 1866, J. H. Ponsonby was, in club matches at least, the complete cricketer, a steady and consistent bat, a wonderfully successful lob bowler and, when required, a competent wicketkeeper. For IZ *v.* the School of Gunnery at Shoeburyness in 1874 he achieved the remarkable feat of taking nineteen wickets in a twelve-a-side match. Even so his figures can hardly have been as sensational as those of F. P. U. Pickering for IZ at Charterhouse in 1875. Charterhouse made 30: IZ replied with 108 and then bowled the school out again (it was a one-day match) for 33. Pickering, otherwise unknown as a bowler, though he played for Sussex as a batsman, took 7 for 0 and 7 for 9 with 'grubs and sneaks pitched anywhere'.

One who almost rivalled J. H. Ponsonby in the amount of IZ

cricket he played was W. E. Denison. He had not been in the eleven at Eton, but developed in army and club cricket into a useful bat and a destructive slow bowler. Later he was for years on the Biennial Committee, where he also acted as 'Match Maker', and was President of MCC in 1892. Another slow bowler who took many wickets for the club in the seventies and eighties was Henry Bruen: he too was a late developer, who had not been in the Harrow XI. For IZ *v.* 14 Military of Ireland at Dublin in 1884 he took 18 for 83 in the two innings, twelve of his victims being stumped by C. C. Clarke.

Many runs too were scored for IZ about this time by P. E. Crutchley, an uncle of Gerald Crutchley. Three cricketers of far greater distinction, all of whom had Blues and represented the Gentlemen, were C. K. Francis, F. E. R. Fryer and A. W. Ridley. Francis, a formidable fast bowler and, in club cricket, no mean bat, played for a few years for Middlesex, after which his work at the Bar left no time for first-class cricket: he became a Metropolitan Police magistrate. Fryer, captain of Cambridge in 1873, was one of the most graceful of batsmen, but like many such required a good, fast wicket and was seldom successful at Lord's: however he scored heavily for IZ and sometimes took wickets with his slows. He was a fine shot. Ridley was one of the best amateur all-rounders of the day – a splendid stroke-player who made 103 for the Gentlemen at Lord's in 1876, for a time the most dangerous lob bowler in England and a magnificent field, especially to his own bowling. He is perhaps best remembered for his part in winning the Varsity match for Oxford in 1875, when he was Captain. Cambridge on a dark, cold, damp day with a sodden ball went in to get 175 and were 114 for 7. At this point W. S. Patterson and H. M. Sims had added 47 and were scoring very fast when, with 14 wanted, Ridley put himself on to bowl. He immediately clean bowled Patterson, a very fine bat. In the next over Sims was well caught on the leg boundary off T. W. Lang, and A. F. Smith, the last man but ostensibly played for his batting, came in so nervous that he could hardly hold his bat to face Ridley's lobs, with 7 runs needed. He played for the third ball to turn: it went straight on and bowled him. Ridley had not much time for first-class cricket afterwards: he played a little for Middlesex and frequently for IZ, for whom in 1881 he scored 204 against the Sappers. Later he was for some years on the Committee.

R. L. ARROWSMITH

10

Some Notable Zingari – II

MANY of the prominent IZ cricketers of the 1880s have already been noticed in the chapter on the club's first-class matches. With the nineties came a big change. Until then, first-class matches had been so few that an amateur, however eminent, had lots of time for club cricket in between and R. A. H. Mitchell, A. G. Steel, the Studds, the Lytteltons and others had appeared constantly for IZ. But the great expansion of the county championship in 1895 altered all this and widened enormously the gap between county and club cricket; from now on anyone who played first-class cricket at all regularly was seldom available for IZ or other clubs, however loyal a member he might be. And so, while for instance R. E. Foster or later Douglas Jardine or Gubby Allen, who seldom if ever played a full season's first-class cricket, were at times to be found in IZ sides, others such as A. C. MacLaren, F. S. Jackson and R. H. Spooner played little for the club. And in this book we are concerned primarily with services rendered to IZ.

Few rendered more than Charles Carlos Clarke, elected in 1880. He met with comparatively little success for Surrey, for whom he played fairly frequently from 1873 to 1882, though he was good enough to score in 1883 65 for the Gentlemen of England *v.* Oxford and 63 for MCC *v.* Kent. But in club cricket he was an extremely useful batsman, a fine field and, if required, a competent wicket-keeper: above all he was a splendid match manager. He was invaluable not only to IZ but also to Free Foresters, MCC and the Silwood Park Cricket Club, which he himself founded and which flourished until 1914. He was also in great demand for country-house matches. A friend once said that, if one had him on one's side, it ensured 'having a good time, as he had always a fund of amusement and kept the ball rolling'. Nor was cricket his only interest: he was said to have hunted with thirty-three packs of hounds and was a good musician and actor, closely associated with the Old Stagers, and he sang the IZ song at the dinner in 1904. For over thirty years he was a member of the Biennial Committee and he was long remembered with affection by his friends.

In many of his matches his scorer was his daughter Marjorie, known as 'Bobbie', who on 20 March 1908 was appointed a member by the Governor. The citation reads, 'Know all I Zingari by these presents that I, by virtue of the Powers in me vested, do hereby give leave and licence to Miss Bobbie Clarke to wear in perpetuity (notwithstanding any vicissitudes to which she may be subject, such as marriage, for instance) the Colours of IZ, in the possession of which she was born and bred, so long as she shall maintain the great principles of that institution, that is to say, to keep her promise, keep her temper, and keep up any substitute for a wicket which she may appoint.' Miss Clarke, who later married a Zingaro, C. H. Cowan, remained understandably proud to the end of her life of this unique distinction and kept the citation in a frame on a table in her drawing-room. She died in 1963 aged seventy-eight.

Two contemporary Hampshire cricketers were destined to play an important part in IZ, F. E. Lacey (later Sir Francis) and Major E. G. Wynyard. Lacey played for Cambridge in 1882 and for Hampshire from 1879 to 1897, captaining them from 1888 to 1893. Unfortunately for him Hampshire did not become a first-class county till 1894, but they frequently played against first-class counties and Lacey's performances in these matches left no doubt about his ability. Against Sussex at Hove in 1882 he made 157 and 50 not out, besides taking eleven wickets, while in 1884 against Kent at Southampton he scored 211 in three hours and followed it with 92 not out, thus narrowly missing the great distinction of being the first man to make a century and a double century in an important match. Better remembered, since it still appears in the records as the highest score ever made in a Minor Counties match, is his 323 not out against Norfolk at Southampton in 1887. A tall man who made full use of his height, he was a fine striker of the ball, particularly in front of the wicket, a good field and a useful slow bowler with a deceptive flight. After 1897 his duties as Secretary at Lord's stopped his county cricket, though he continued to play for IZ. As Secretary he did a splendid job, especially in dropping the old easy-going attitude and adopting a more business-like approach. Inevitably this did not please everybody, but there can be no doubt about its benefit to the club. On his retirement in 1926 when he was appointed a Trustee, he was knighted, thus becoming the first man to be honoured specifically for his services to cricket. He had been a member of the IZ Committee since 1900 and in 1914 succeeded A. G. Steel as Liberal Legal Adviser; for many years he was also Secretary.

Major E. G. Wynyard, known to his friends as Teddy, played a vast quantity of cricket for IZ over many years; he continued to run sides for the club till he was nearer seventy than sixty and remained on the Committee till his death. His contemporaries were unanimous that, had he been able to play first-class cricket uninterruptedly in his prime, he would have been remembered among the great, but he was thirty-three when Hampshire became first-class and forty-two when he retired from the army, so his opportunities were severely restricted. None the less he represented England against Australia at the Oval in 1896, a year when the competition for places as batsmen was fierce. For him personally the match was somewhat of a disappointment. It was played throughout on an extremely difficult wicket and Wynyard, going in at about ten past six on the second evening and not out at the close, reckoned he had never batted better in his life and hoped to make some runs next morning. However W. G., who was Captain, came out, pressed a huge thumb on the pitch and said, 'Sorry, you must all be out in half an hour. We must have them in by twelve-thirty at latest.' At this point England were 60 for 5, only 86 ahead. They were all out for 84 and Australia, with a tremendous batting side seven of whom made their thousand runs that year, were left to get 111 with unlimited time to do it. Against Peel, slow left, and J. T. Hearne, medium right, they were 14 for 7 and only some spirited hitting by McKibbin, the last man, enabled them to reach 44. No wonder Wynyard regarded W.G. as incomparably the best captain he had ever known. A few weeks earlier Wynyard had played a superb innings of 268 against Yorkshire, the champion county; it took him six hours and he scored exactly two-thirds of the runs made while he was in. In the first-class averages that season he came second to Ranji, scoring 1038 runs with an average of fractionally under 50. A splendid attacking bat, he had a complete armoury of strokes and, in an age when amateurs especially tended to look for their runs mainly on the off, he was equally strong on the leg and particularly expert at the pull, played as W.G. and George Hirst used to play it, by dropping on his right knee and taking the ball at the pitch from just outside the off stump over or wide of mid-on. He was a fine driver and, if the bowler shortened his length, would cut or hook him. Left-handers he constantly drove for four over extra-cover or cover. He was a brilliant field anywhere, an adequate wicketkeeper in a crisis and a good enough lob bowler to pick up quite a few wickets even in first-class cricket. He was twice asked to go to Australia, by Stoddart in 1897, when the War Office refused him leave, and by the MCC, desperate to find a captain, in 1907. Again he was unable to accept, this time perhaps luckily. It is difficult to believe that at forty-six, when he had more or less dropped out of county cricket, he would really have been up to Test match form. Apart from his cricket he had been a member of the Old Carthusian side which won the FA Cup in 1881 and he had also won the International Toboggan Race at Davos Platz in 1896. He was a natural athlete.

Running club sides as a veteran, he inspired considerable awe; indeed Sir John Masterman, who although thirty years his junior was a close friend, wrote, 'As a captain the word martinet is too weak to express his dominant personality.' Once captaining IZ *v.* Lords and Commons, he overheard his two natural opening bowlers discussing in a friendly style which of them ought to have the advantage of the stiff breeze which was blowing straight down the wicket. Wynyard solved the problem by opening the bowling downwind himself with his lobs and, to do him justice, all but clean bowled that beautiful batsman the Hon. Clarence Bruce, later Lord Aberdare, in the first over. Again, if a young player suggested too positively that the right place for him to bat was three or four, he was apt to find himself relegated to number eleven. It was not to be expected that such a forceful character would be a docile member of a committee and Sir Francis Lacey sending to the Governor, who had been unavoidably absent, an account of a meeting in April 1934, concluded, 'They are good boys your IZ officers. Even Teddy submitted to order.' If such characters are rarer now, life is doubtless more peaceful, but it is by no means certain that it is better.

Captaining Yorkshire from 1883 to 1910, Lord Hawke had had little chance of playing much for IZ, but he was a keen Zingaro and served on the committee from the end of the First World War until his death. What is more, the meetings were constantly held at his house in Belgrave Square, where the hospitality was princely. The generally received theory was that a candidate who was considered after lunch had a better chance of success than one whose name had come up earlier.

To Billy Findlay, IZ owes an immense debt. I have always understood that it was he more than anyone else who was responsible for putting new life into the club in the later 1920s. Captain of Eton and Oxford, a good wicketkeeper who kept for Lancashire when they were county champions in 1904, and a sound bat, he was Secretary at the Oval from 1907 to 1920, Assistant Secretary at Lord's from 1920 to 1926 and then Secretary till 1936; later he became a Trustee of MCC and was President in 1951–2. After retiring from Lord's he lived in Kent and was an outstanding Chief of the Band of Brothers from 1946 to his death in 1953. At one time he was on the committee of four county cricket clubs simultaneously, Lancashire, Surrey, Kent and Middlesex. For years he was on the IZ Committee; he succeeded Sir Francis Lacey as Secretary and was himself succeeded by our present Treasurer, Ronny Aird. On a committee his charm, his courtesy and his efficiency were great assets, but an even greater in clubs like IZ and BB was his determination to maintain a high standard of membership. He was fond of saying: 'To miss a good man is a misfortune, to elect a bad man is a disaster.' I had always supposed that he was himself the author of this adage, but I now find that it was used by the Governor in his foreword to the 1929 IZ book, so it may really be Lord Dartmouth's or may of course be older. At any rate it was the principle on which Billy worked and long experience has convinced me of its wisdom. He had a delightful precision of speech and gift of understatement. As an example which I have always treasured of the refinements of a bygone age, I once asked him if what I had been told myself by older members was true, that one should never wear an IZ tie in a bar – if one was staying in a hotel, one should ring for the waiter to bring one a drink, not go and look for it oneself. Billy's reply was, 'I don't think it would be – very acceptable.' Looking back, I find that I am unable to imagine Billy himself in even the most respectable bar, whatever tie he might have been wearing.

Brigadier Willie Clark, who was one of his chief supporters in revitalizing IZ, was on the Committee for some forty years and during many of them Custos Rotulorum. He had ceased to play by the time I knew him, though he still ran matches, but he had, I believe, been a good wicketkeeper. On a committee he was invaluable; he always spoke his mind clearly and forcibly on any subject or any candidate about whom he held strong views, never worrying in case he might be offending some of his fellows, and though obviously sometimes one might not agree with him, his opinion was never one to be lightly dismissed. At the same time, he was never tiresomely obstructive (an important point in a club one of whose rules for election has always been, 'one straight ball to exclude') and if the feeling of the meeting was clearly against him, he would gracefully withdraw his objection, without of course retracting his opinion. He would never have behaved like one member of the Committee whom Sir John Masterman could recall, who, when a candidate of his had been rejected, steadfastly blackballed every subsequent candidate at that particular meeting.

After he had retired from the army, Willie gave much time to the Scout movement, but his main recreation was setting in order the lists of members, past and present, of cricket clubs. The two on which he spent most time were IZ and Foresters, both of which now have, thanks to him, a full list from the beginning, complete with Christian names, titles or ranks and exact dates of birth and death. Other clubs whose lists he tackled included BB, on which he was working for the second time when he died, Oxford Authentics and Hampshire Hogs; nor can I be certain that this list is complete. On all these at any rate I was happy and honoured to be able to help him, and I can say without hesitation that he was a very remarkable researcher indeed, patient, methodical and accurate, prepared to write endless letters in order to get information and wholly undeterred by obstacles which would have halted a less determined man. One member, of whom nothing had been heard for many years, had a brother living who was an admiral. Willie wrote to the Admiral and asked where his brother was. The Admiral replied rather huffily that his brother had been dead some years. Most of us would have assumed such an answer to be true. Not so Willie: he wrote to the Admiral saying he did not believe him and would he please tell him where he was. The Admiral then admitted that his brother was alive, but refused to give any further information. Ironically a year or two later the man's death, at some apparently respectable address in London, appeared in *The Times*. Willie lived at Chislehurst in a house full of priceless furniture, which he bequeathed to the Victoria and Albert. Until he was over ninety he came up to London by train six days a week to lunch at the 'Rag', of which he had been a member so long that he did not pay a subscription. Unless he had some engagement later, he would return in the early afternoon.

Another who served thirty or more years on the Committee at this period was Sir John Masterman, known to his countless friends as 'J.C.', one of the most versatile men of his generation. He was for many years a Don at Christ Church; he was pressed in 1933 to stand for the headmastership of Eton but felt that in fact he was better suited to University life, and eventually became an outstanding Provost of his old college, Worcester. As if this were not enough, after retiring from the Provostship at the age of seventy, he spent six years as personnel adviser to a large industrial company, Birfield. During the Second World War he worked for MI5 and later wrote a fascinating and highly controversial account of the work there under the title of *Double Cross*. He was also author of a number of other books, one of which, *Fate Cannot Harm Me*, contains a brilliant account of a country-house cricket match, while his autobiography, *On the Chariot Wheel*, has an interesting passage on IZ. He was himself a remarkable games player. As an undergraduate his main athletic distinction had been to win the high jump in the Varsity sports. Later he won several international caps at hockey, represented England against both Scotland and Ireland at lawn tennis and competed many times at Wimbledon with considerable success, played in the amateur championships at squash and was a low-handicap golfer and a member of the Oxford and Cambridge Golfing Society. As a cricketer he had the comparatively rare distinction of being elected a Harlequin years after he had gone down, played both for them and the Foresters against Oxford University and for a couple of seasons was a useful member of the Oxfordshire side. If not quite a first-class player, he was for years a tower of strength to club sides, a steady right-hand medium-pace bowler, a pretty heavy-scoring left-hand bat and a good catcher in the slips. Curiously enough no one watching him bat or bowl would have guessed that he was a great natural games player. With slightly hunched shoulders, he had a somewhat clumsy action and certainly did not make full use of his height, but he could bowl with great accuracy for long periods and, without ever being deadly, took his full share of wickets. His batting too was rather ungainly, but, if he crouched a bit, his head was well over the ball and he gave the impression of watching it right onto the bat: moreover his bat was impeccably straight. Perhaps no man has ever proposed more candidates, whether for IZ or Foresters. He and Willie Clark both received the Freedom of the club for their services.

There are no logical grounds for supposing that cricket attracts a larger number of eccentrics than other games, but there is no doubt that, owing to the length of time a match takes and the opportunities for conversation on and off the field, there is no game in which a man has such opportunities of displaying his eccentricities. Of eccentrics IZ has had probably neither more nor less than its due share and

D.R. Jardine

G.O.B. Allen

P.B.H. May

M.C. Cowdrey

IZ v

(*Left to right*) (*Standing*): umpire: R. Needham; R.F.S. Miles,
M.C.T. Prichard, A. Rice, A.M. Douglass, D.G. Bishop (IZ) J. Smith,
T.A.L. Huskinson (IZ), N.C.D. Craig (IZ), J.S. Knox (IZ),
G.W.G. Philipps, R.I. Evans (IZ), B. Smallwood, R.J. Priestley (IZ)
I. MacDonald (IZ), H.M. Wyndham (IZ), umpire.

Hunts, 1972.

(*Sitting*) Sir William Becher, Bt, S.G. Metcalfe, R.L. Arrowsmith, J.C.R. Downing (captain), Lord Cobham, A.S.R. de W. Winlaw (IZ captain), J.T. Morgan, M. Tindall (IZ), C.J. Lee, B.G. Brocklehurst (IZ)

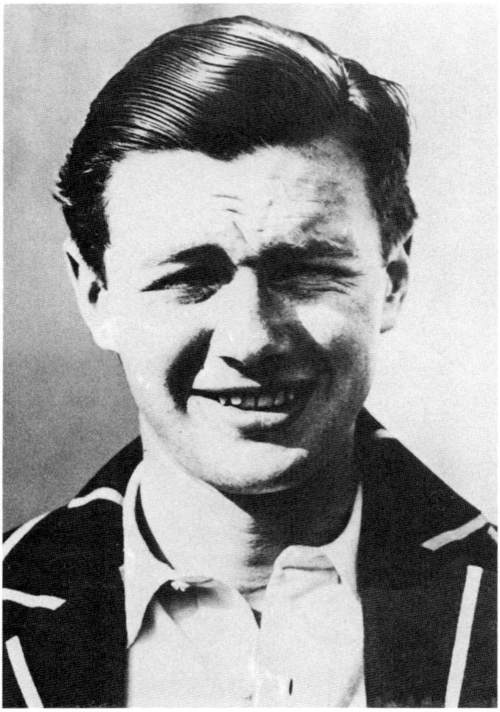

J.H. Pawle

Lord Porchester

Highclere cricket ground

Spectators at Arundel, 1981
– Lord Cornwallis, Lady Becher, Lord Home, Lady Home,
Sir William Becher, Bt, R. Aird, (*standing*) R.L. Arrowsmith

IZ v. Green Jackets Club, St Cross 27 June 1981.
(*Left to right*) Sir Charles Mott-Radclyffe, Brig. P.M. Welsh,
Gen. Sir Edwin Bramall, A.E.L. Hill, Sir William Becher, Bt,
Maj. C.J. Wilson, R.J. Priestley (captain, IZ), Col. C.C. Dunphie
(captain Green Jackets Club)

C.S. Crawley

Sir William Becher, Bt

R.L. Arrowsmith

B.J.W. Hill

Camden Park, Menangle, NSW, where IZ Australia have played much cricket

IZ Australia v. Hampshire Hogs at Warnford, 1977.
(*Left to right*) P. Coleman, J.R. Hoyle, R. Coleman, S.W. White, T.R.H. Savill, R.B. Tubbs, M.T. McKaughan, A.M. Orr, P.V. James (*hidden*), B.A. Eastment, E.G. Wiles

Lord Home of the Hirsel
– Governor 4th Wicket Down

IZ v. Royal Regiment of Fusiliers played
on the Aldershot Officers Club Ground 12 June 1982.
(*From left to right*) (*Standing*) D.J.C. Faber,
R.S.A. Paget Steavenson, M.R. Cooper, J.P. Boden, A.T. Fennell,
A.E. Martin Smith, R.H. Purser, D.R. Fyfe-Jamieson.
(*Sitting*) P.G. Lowndes, C.J.H. Green, C.E.P. Carter, (captain RR of Fusiliers),
C.J.T. Holland (captain IZ) Maj. N.J.P. Brunt, Maj. J.O. Hopkins.
C.E.P. Carter, Maj. N.J.P. Brunt, Maj. J.O. Hopkins are members
of RR of Fusiliers and also members of IZ

it would be invidious, even if it were possible, to attempt to compile a list of them. But if one may choose one out of many, none perhaps has better claims than Gerry Weigall, not only because he features frequently in books of reminiscences which deal with his period, but because he was a very loyal Zingaro, one of six Zingaric brothers, and because he was an active playing member for fifty years. He played his first match for IZ in 1889, the year of his election, and he was still playing regular club cricket in 1939 and, but for the war, would doubtless have gone on longer. Nor was he even then a passenger. I remember playing with him in 1935 in a charity match for Tich Freeman against Ashford, then one of the strongest clubs in Kent. Tich had had some disappointments, which doubtless accounted for my presence, and to crown all Arthur Fagg failed to turn up. This left our batting rather fragile and we were only saved from disgrace by Gerry who, having fielded on the boundary for most of the Ashford innings with the agility of a man half his age, now contributed 40 or 50, and then got me to drive him round to the Ashford Club to give a squash lesson to a member of the opposition before dinner – not bad for a man of sixty-five. Five years earlier he had come out to field as substitute for Kent against the Australians at Canterbury without noticeably lowering the standard.

He had in his prime been a first-class player, though never near the top of the first class. He had played in two extremely strong Cambridge sides, both of which contained six men who appeared at some time for the Gentlemen at Lord's (one had in addition to these a wicketkeeper who played in a Test against Australia, but never for the Gentlemen) and he had for some years been a fairly regular member of the Kent side and made a reasonable number of runs for them. He was almost entirely an off-side batsman, a beautiful cutter and a good off-driver: his nearest approach to a leg-side stroke was a tickle round the corner. The hook he regarded with horror, as he did the back shot played square-on facing the bowler: both he attributed to the introduction of the box. 'Never hook,' he would say, 'until you have made eighty-four.' Though he took a general interest in all games, was a keen racing man and a devotee of the theatre, his life centred on cricket, with rackets (which he had played for Cambridge) and squash as runners-up. What else he had ever done in life was somewhat of a mystery. At one time he was certainly on the Stock Exchange, though it is hard to imagine anyone entrusting his money to one so clearly incapable of keeping any money of his own. He had two spells as coach to the Kent County Cricket Club, but despite his undoubted knowledge of cricket technique and his enthusiasm, he was not a success. Moreover his absences from duty became longer and more frequent until at last the Committee had to dispense with his services. Even this did not deter him from applying a few years later for the vacant post of Manager and indeed from being confident that he would be appointed. He wrote a good deal for the papers and at one period used actually to report matches for *The Times*. One shudders to think of the amount of correction which these must have entailed for someone: he had little idea of the construction of an English sentence and none whatever of punctuation. For years an advertisement used to appear in *Wisden* for Wisden's squash balls:

G. J. V. Weigall writes, 'The best ball for a standard size court is one with a small hole in it about 15/8 in. It is black all through and has no ear in it to get loose and rattle inside the ball after having played with it for a short time, like the solid ball. . . . The bound of the ball is seldom higher than the knee, and at the same time goes well off the back wall. Anyone who builds very large courts and has a return board 6 in. from the ground a fast ball may be possible. . . .'

Yet he is best remembered for his aphorisms. 'Never run to cover.' I had this twice in two overs. He and I were batting together and he drove hard and straight to cover. I knew my man, shouted firmly 'No' before he could call 'Yes' and stood my ground. This did not stop him starting up the wicket; he turned, just got in on his pads, rose, dusted himself, beamed at me and said, 'Quite right: never run to cover.' In the next over I myself hit one straight to cover and immediately shouted 'No.' To my horror I saw Gerry again two or three yards down the wicket. Again he just got in on his pads and I felt it was my turn then to say, 'Never run to cover.' He had always been a notoriously bad runner and in the 'Varsity match of 1892, when his 63 not out was easily the highest score in a total of 160, he undid much of the good he had done by running out those two great batsmen F. S. Jackson and C. M. Wells. Tradition has it that meeting Jackson, his captain, who played for England the next summer, in the middle of the wicket he said, 'Go back, Jacker: I'm set.' In the course of Gerry's innings another fine batsman, A. J. L. Hill, was also run out, but in this case there was some doubt which of them was to blame. Another of his sayings was, 'Never eat pie at a cricket lunch.' This was before the days of refrigerators. Once, when MCC were playing Bradfield, the first course was steak and kidney pie. All eyes were on Gerry and he had to refuse it. Apple pie followed. Again all eyes were on Gerry, whose lunch perforce was confined to salad and cheese and biscuits. 'Never play back at the bottom end at Canterbury' – this was said to me while we were waiting to bat for a BB side which was in sore trouble against Alan Watt and Arthur Blunden. Almost immediately Gerry went in, played back at the bottom end, and his stumps were scattered. And so one might go on.

Yet people who, knowing Gerry only superficially, regarded him merely as a figure of fun were wrong. He had in fact a deep knowledge of cricket and his wildest exaggerations were for the most part exaggerations of the truth. If too often he had just seen 'the finest natural bowler since Sidney Barnes, sir' or 'the most beautiful off-side player since Lionel Palairet', one knew that he had seen a bowler or batsman of real possibilities, even if these possibilities were not always fulfilled. When on the other hand he called Leyland, destined to be one of our greatest Test match batsmen, 'a cross-bat village-greener' and Mead 'a leaden-footed carthorse', it was not to be taken as serious criticism: it was his way of expressing his disgust that they had been preferred to his idol Frank Woolley for a tour to Australia. One could forgive much to such an enthusiast. Moreover he never said an unkind thing about anyone. Perhaps the nearest he ever came to doing so was when he described our late Governor's decision (taken on the advice of his opening bowlers) to put the Australians in at Worcester as the most monstrous thing since the Crucifixion. He certainly showed at times a real gift for words, as when he described a tall, dark, sinuous colonial bowler with curious-coloured eyes as 'that green-eyed ant-eater'. Much too that he said, especially about himself, was said with a chuckle and with his tongue in his cheek and was not meant to be taken too seriously – 'All my words are golden, sir,' or 'There are only three people who know anything about cricket, Archie MacLaren, Charles Fry and myself, and I know more than the other two.'

Some of us still miss that slight, active, mustachioed figure dressed usually in a dark brown suit, with a bowler hat in winter and a straw boater with IZ ribbon in summer, carrying a neatly rolled umbrella, which was used less as a protection against rain than to illustrate a stroke in whatever game he was talking about at the moment – and that game was generally cricket.

R. L. ARROWSMITH

11

I Zingari Australia

PROMPTNESS is not one of the virtues of the Australian Zingaro. It is rare for his team to be at the ground by the appointed hour and when it is, the full complement not infrequently turns out to be 10 or 12. This failing can be traced back to the beginnings of the club. In 1878 Australia sent its first team to England and such was the interest that cricket teams were springing up like mushrooms. A Sydney lawyer, George F. Evans, decided that he should form a club. He presented his case to a small gathering at his father's gracious residence in the heart of present-day Kings Cross and the verdict was to call the new infant the Iona Cricket Club. The influential founders were then able to persuade the Governor of New South Wales, the Rt. Hon. C. R. B. Carrington, to become its Patron, and a former Premier of New South Wales, Sir Patrick Jennings, to be its first President.

The decision had now been made but, with an outstanding example of IZ procrastination, it was not for another two years, in 1888, that the first match was actually played. Iona lost that match by 'nine wickets and 4 runs', having managed only 37 and 28 in its two innings. Hardly an auspicious debut for a club now in the nervous nineties but thanks to some fleet footwork by the Committee, the club reappeared a fortnight later under the name I Zingari. The change was for the better, for the renamed club recorded its first victory, by 37 runs.

There had been an I Zingari Club in Victoria in the 1850s, which indicates that the name had quickly become known in the colonies. This club's existence was, however, shortlived. The new club decided that its name should be sanctioned by I Zingari in England. Colonel H. W. Renny-Tailyour, a British Army officer stationed in Sydney, who frequently played with the club, advised the Committee that he would endeavour to arrange affiliation with I Zingari when he returned to England. He approached the Rt Hon. Sir Spencer Ponsonby Fane, a personal friend and Governor of the club, on his arrival. Permission to use the name 'I Zingari' was given provided the word 'Australia' was added. Permission was also given to adopt black, red and gold as the club colours.

By the start of the second season the nets at the Association Ground (now the Sydney Cricket Ground) were full of activity. 'With the exception of Zingari,' the *Evening News* reported, 'the whole of the clubs were fairly well represented.' Clearly the members were displaying the same enthusiasm for practice as their successors do now. It is equally clear, however, that the club was being accepted as one of the senior clubs in Sydney cricket, and it was soon fielding five teams. In 1892 the performances of its senior team were good enough for it to enter the senior competition conducted by the New South Wales Cricket Association. Two years later Grade cricket – with its strict residential qualifications – was introduced and the senior clubs were disbanded.

IZ reverted to purely social matches and began to establish a series of associations that continue today. The great public schools were added to the fixture list, and is there not a familiar ring in the King's School magazine's comment on the IZ batting in the first match? 'Their commencement was inauspicious, their first three wickets falling for four runs'? Things weren't much better in the following year's fixtures: 'I Zingari were short and three of our third eleven played with them and these, strange to say, made nearly all their runs.'

Fixtures with the army and navy also started in the 1890s. The early Zingaro was a hardy fellow, for, in a match against the Artillery, the *Evening News* noted, 'The enthusiasm of these two teams was more than the rain could damp and they played even without the protection of umbrellas.'

It was in this same decade that the club, in keeping with its name, began venturing to the country centres of New South Wales. These matches were sufficiently popular to draw crowds of several hundreds even if the cricketing correspondent of the Maitland newspaper was inclined to be a trifle choleric about one IZ team. 'Their fielding was none too safe. The wicketkeeper was not first class . . . the less said about their batting the better.' Even the poor old IZ umpire was chastised as being 'rather too fleshy to take an active part in the game'. And for anyone who regards chucking as a modern phenomenon, a 'prominent member of the Zingari team' confided to the *Scone Advocate* 'that Howell, Trumble and McLeod are the only three fair bowlers in the colonies at present. McKibbin, Jones and even Noble all throw more or less'!

In Sydney the press was somewhat more generous in its praise of IZ's score of 396 for 6 against Double Bay in 1896.

> None of the six were bowled, the Double Bay umpiring being mainly responsible for the five wickets that fell. One batsman was given out l.b.w. to a ball bowled round the wicket . . . and two others were given caught off the first bounce of the ball. At 4.30 the I Zingaris closed their innings, or it is possible the side would have put up a record score for the oval which at present stands at 486, which by the way was put up by the I Zingari.

The stalwart of the early years was Dr P. C. Charlton, later to become the club's Patron-in-Perpetuity. He had represented Australia as a member of W. L. Murdoch's team in England in 1890 and even when playing for IZ in 1897 was selected for the New South Wales XI. A contemporary newspaper remarked that 'Charlton plays lolly-pop cricket', a distasteful observation to many IZ cricketers who continue to play beyond their years in the hope that history may repeat itself.

It is true that crowds of 300 no longer turn up to an IZ match and the present player has to be content with a couple of stray dogs and perhaps an unwilling wife dragooned to help with lunch and tea. But, otherwise, the pattern and characteristics of IZ cricket have changed little in the period that followed the founding years. The country tours have been extended to include Melbourne and Brisbane, and three tours to New Zealand have been made. In 1977, the club's ninetieth year, a team toured England, one of the highlights being the first cricketing encounter with the club that started it all. Appropriately, the parent won.

At home, up to eighty fixtures a year are arranged. Regular weekly matches for two IZ teams are played in the Sydney metropolitan area, and there is frequently a third fixture at lovely Camden Park, thirty miles from Sydney and birthplace of the Australian wool industry. Here teams from the UK, Canada, India, Hong Kong, Sri Lanka, Malaysia and New Zealand have been entertained.

The club first played at Camden Park in 1895 when the members were 'hospitably entertained by the Messrs Onslow'. In 1969 the club leased an area of land from Quentin Macarthur Stanham, a member of the club and a descendant of the Messrs Onslow, and built its own oval and pavilion among the gum trees on this historic property. Many well-known cricketers have appeared here with or against IZ. A cricket ball is still lodged sixty feet up a gum tree, the reminder of a towering six by Doug Walters. The late Bert Oldfield umpired in the first match, and not too distantly the club's President, Martin Donnelly, pulled a hamstring sprinting round the boundary at a time when all his cricketing contemporaries would long since have hung up their boots.

There are now 177 members of IZ Australia. They are drawn from many walks of life and over the years have included a sprinkling of former international and state players like H. H. Massie, Dr H. V. Hordern, E. C. S. White, J. W. Burke, I. D. Craig, G. Goonesena, R. G. Archer and M. P. Donnelly. The much larger component of the membership is a happy band of lesser sportsmen whose main attributes are the enjoyment of good cricket and the bonds of friendship which cricket alone can bring. People like Bill Douglass who, when he isn't preparing the wicket at Camden or attending a Centenary Test, still executes his famous but indescribable stroke to third man which has made him IZ's leading runscorer. Or Graham Wright who, to mark his sixtieth birthday during a tour of New Zealand, was promoted from number eleven to number three and batted through the innings. Or Eric Siddeley, whose record of seven hat tricks is unlikely ever to be broken. Or perhaps a younger member like Richard Lee who, in the latest season, has taken ten wickets in an innings. . . .

I Zingari Australia looks forward to 1988. That year marks the bicentenary of the founding of Australia. It also marks the centenary of one of the oldest clubs in Australia still playing cricket in the spirit in which, it believes, it was designed to be played.

J. M. ELDERSHAW

APPENDIX I

From the IZ Book

ORIGIN

When at Cambridge, F. Ponsonby, C. Taylor, W. Bolland and others devoted some of their leisure moments to Cricket and Theatricals. Hence sprang many Matches under various names, several Private Theatrical Meetings and, in 1842, the annual Canterbury Gatherings of Old Stagers.

In July 1845, F. Ponsonby, S. Ponsonby, J. L. Baldwin and R. P. Long (who under mesmeric influence assisted at the séance) found themselves at supper at the Blenheim Hotel, Bond Street. They then and there formed a Club, christened the same; framed Rules, and the following day informed W. Bolland that he was Perpetual President, and twenty of their friends that they were Members of I Zingari.

* * *

ORIGINAL MEMBERS

Perpetual President
Bolland, W. P.

Annual Vice-President
Baldwin, J. L.

Biennial Committee

Bessborough, 6th Earl of
Cavendish-Bentinck, Rt Hon. G. A. F.
Morse, Charles
Nethercote, H. O.
Ponsonby Fane, Rt Hon. Sir S. C. B.
Taylor, C. G.

Members

Broughton, R. J. P.
Dewing, E. M.
Gambier, Maj.-Gen. Gloucester
Hartopp, E. S. E.
Leslie, Sir John, Bt
Loftus, Lord H. Y. A.
Mills, Rev. B. S. T.
Pickering, Rev. J. H.
Pickering, W. P.
Randolph, Rev. Cyril
Sheppard, J. G.
Strathmore, 12th Earl of
Strathmore, 13th Earl of
Wellesley, R. G.

Treasurer and Auditor
Grimston, Hon. Robert

Liberal Legal Adviser
Taylor, Tom

Secretary
Long, R. P.

HISTORY OF PRESENT POSITION

That was the small beginning of a great Club which numbers now well over one thousand members.

The objects of the Club in the first instance were Cricket and Acting.

In their search for a home the Founders fastened on Canterbury. They had been the Founders too, of the Great Canterbury Cricket Week, which, in spite of many changes, still holds its own as one of the most popular gatherings of the cricketing year.

In the early years of the Canterbury Week its last two days were devoted to a Zingaric Match.

When cricket became a more serious business, other changes followed. IZ, as far as cricket was concerned, was gradually crowded out, but as its cricket waned the acting waxed, and today the Old Stagers are among the greatest exponents of amateur acting.

IN THE CANTERBURY WEEK

The Old Stagers and I Zingari walk ever hand in hand,
And through the week our colours blend as side by side we stand.
Alas! IZ's been crowded out, no matches now we play,
But we treasure grateful memories in the true Zingaric way.

And though today IZ is no longer active in the 'Flesh', the 'Spirit' of IZ is as active as ever.

Here is the message of the 'Spirit' of IZ in 1928. It is well worth record.

There's a motto of our Order every cricketer should know,
And whatever fate or fortune has in store,
It will help you in your wanderings as through the world you go,
If you always keep this motto to the fore.
When luck seems all against you and everything looks blue,
And there's nothing left to do but grin and stick it,
You must always keep your temper, you must keep your promise too
And throughout the game of life keep up your wicket.

This is the Spirit of I Zingari. The Spirit that inspired our Founders in the old days. The Spirit that is with us today. The Spirit that will remain with us till 'Time' (and the Canterbury Cricket Week) shall be no more.

THE BOOKS

There is a 'Book', and there are 'Books'.

The 'Book' is one that should be in the hands of every Member. It gives the rules of the Club, the regulations of the Club, the aspirations of the Club, and Members of the Club of all sorts and conditions, and much other valuable information.

But 'The Books' are different. For many years Scrap Books were kept by the first Governor. They are interesting, and with others they have now, thanks to the courtesy of the MCC, found a domicile at Lord's.

SONG OF I ZINGARI
WRITTEN BY
THE PERPETUAL PRESIDENT

Air – 'Red, White and Blue'

We are told England's armies assembled
When Liberty's cause was in view;
We are told too that tyranny trembled
'Neath the folds of the Red, White and Blue.
Yes! The Red, White and Blue o'er the ocean
Has floated in conquests of old,
But tonight let us pledge our devotion
To the folds of the Black, Red and Gold.

Chorus: To the folds, etc. etc.

The ball the stout cricketer urges,
Cleaves a pathway of peace o'er the plain,
The weapon he wields leaves no scourges,
No record of carnage or pain;
No! 'Tis to cement man's affection,
Reviving his pastime of old.
In our camp then we fear no defection.
From the folds of the Black, Red and Gold.

Chorus: From the folds, etc. etc.

As the eagle scans desert and mountain,
As the sea-bird the wilds of the deep,
As the water springs free from the fountain,
And dashes unbound down the steep,
So our wandering band shuns all warning,
In every soil plants its hold,
Each tract of Old England adorning
With the folds of the Black, Red and Gold.

Chorus: With the folds, etc. etc.

For to-night is the night of all others,
And our Song like a knot firmly tied,
Unites all our Wandering Brothers
Who are scattered today far and wide.
Out of darkness, through fire, into light,
Is the story our Colours have told.
Let us keep then our goal full in sight
From the Black, through the Red, to the Gold.

Chorus: From the Black, etc. etc.

Then the wine cup, the wine cup bear hither
Fill high, we sip nought but the brim,
May the germ we have planted ne'er wither,
Nor the star of our birthright grow dim;
May the friendships we've formed never sever,
May each link lengthen long and grow old,
In a bumper, 'Here's Cricket for ever,'
'Neath the folds of the Black, Red and Gold.

Chorus: 'Neath the folds, etc. etc.

RULES AND REGULATIONS

At a Meeting held – no matter when, and much less where – NOBODY, Chairman.

The following Rules and Regulations were proposed and unanimously adopted:

'Resolved,'

1. That a Club be founded for mutual Cricket accommodation, which shall have the name and style of 'I Zingari'.

2. That the Club be under the control of a Perpetual President, an Annual Vice President, a Governor, and other Officers.

3. That no Candidate be proposed unless so agreed at a meeting consisting of the PP, AVP, and not less than two Officers. The mode of election as follows: The Candidate shall be placed at a wicket, with or without a bat, as the Officers may decide, and be bowled at by the AVP, or by any Member of IZ so deputed by the AVP. One straight ball to exclude. The number of balls given not to exceed the number of Members comprising IZ (Altered, see Rule 14).

4. That every Member have the privilege of playing one match during the season, when upon his producing five names of Members (in addition to his own) who are willing to take part in such match, five other Members shall be bound in honour to make up the team.

5. That the field be under the SOLE control of the Member making the match, or any Zingaro whom he may depute.

6. That the Entrance be nothing, and the Annual Subscription do not exceed the Entrance, but that the expenses of a match (i.e. of the Zingaric umpire, etc.) be defrayed by the Members engaged therein.

7. That all directions connected with the game *may* be conveyed in the French or Italian languages.

(8. THAT NO MEMBER UPON ANY OCCASION PLAY AS AN OPPONENT TO IZ, EXCEPT WITH THE PERMISSION OF THE GOVERNOR IN VERY SPECIAL CIRCUMSTANCES. ANY TRANSGRESSION OF THIS RULE TO ENTAIL IMMEDIATE EXPULSION FROM THE CLUB.) By a resolution of the Biennial Committee on 17 December 1970, this rule was suspended *sine die*.

9. That, although mirth be acceptable upon all occasions, ill-timed mirth be generally avoided, and that all personalities, particularly those postprandial, be evaded.

10. That the PP, AVP, and not less than two Officers be empowered to frame such additional rules or regulations as they may deem conducive to the welfare of IZ, provided always that they do not cancel former rules or regulations.

11. That the AVP be empowered to depute a substitute in the place of any absent Officer.

12. When matches are arranged with the Royal Navy or any portion of it, the Household Brigade, the Green Jackets, the Staff College, RE, RA, or any Regiment, Members of IZ selected to play for the opposing Team shall not be subject to Rule 8.

13. That in future NO questions of ANY KIND be put to the PP, AVP or to the Officers.

14. That the number of the Club be limited . . . See Rule 13.

15. That the Colours of IZ, be Black, Red and Gold. That they may be worn also by the Wives, Daughters, and Sisters of IZ.

16. That a Twenty-two may be selected as Candidates, who, *Sibenesegesserint*, may be hereafter elected.

N.B. – Candidates will not wear the Colours of IZ, nor will they be subject to Rule 8.

17. Any interpretations of the foregoing Rules are in the hands of the Governor.

THE FREEDOM

The Freedom of the Club is the highest honour the Club has to bestow. It is very rarely given.

In bygone days, when an Irish tour was always part of the Club's programme, IZ were entertained by the Lord Lieutenant of Ireland at the Vice-regal Lodge. In recognition of his hospitality it was customary for the Freedom of the Club to be presented to him with due pomp and ceremony.

In later times after the Irish tour had been discontinued it was desired to give the honour a more extended application. Consequently the Freedom has occasionally been conferred on certain distinguished men who have given outstanding service to the Commonwealth.

SIBENES

Number 16 of the original rules reads 'That a Twenty-Two may be selected as Candidates, who, *Sibenesegesserint*, may be hereafter elected.'

In old days, the Sibenes, never very numerous, were the sons of friends of the Governor. They became 'Candidates' frequently at a very early age. They remained 'Candidates' till, without further ceremony, they passed on to become Members.

We have now made the candidature really probative, in the hopes that the Sibenes will join with us in showing the cricketing world the spirit in which the game ought to be played.

So these Sibenes have to earn promotion. Promotion is not difficult if the true spirit is really there. Sibenes are expected to play as often as they can for the Club. They do *not* wear the Colours of the Club nor are they subject to Rule 8.

Since the Sibenes do not wear IZ Colours they are free to wear what other colours they like when playing for the Club, and as they are not subject to Rule 8, it is open to them to play for 'the other side', though this privilege should be exercised with discretion.

It should be borne in mind that the duty of a Sibene to the Club does not end when he has earned promotion. It is only a beginning. Our hope is that in learning how to follow he will learn how to lead, and will become in his turn a dependable Member of the Old Club.

THE COLOURS

The Colours are Black, Red and Gold.

Members are reminded that 'Out of darkness, through fire, into light,' is the foundation on which the Colours of IZ are built. It is most important that the Colours should always be worn showing the Gold at top.

The Colours are worn by Members, their 'Wives', 'Widows', 'Daughters' and 'Sisters', but not by 'Sibenes'.

By long and sacred custom 'Old Stagers' wear the Colours during Canterbury Week.

On collar days the sash is worn outside the waistcoat, from the right shoulder to left hip.

The official colours can be obtained from Messrs Beale & Inman, 131 New Bond Street, W1.

INFORMATION

The Officers, anxious to meet the views of the Club in general, and of some Members in particular, beg to say should any information be required, the Member or Members desirous of such information may obtain it (if he or they can) by a written application to the Chairman, who presided at the formation of the Club, or to the Governor, who may or may not reply.

'A match list, on which relevant information is given, is issued as early as possible in the year. Copies may be obtained by personal application to the Auditor, or by enclosing a stamped and addressed envelope to him at Lord's.' – MEMBERS PLEASE NOTE

OBSERVATION

Rule 8 transgressed upon *two occasions only* – Immediate expulsion the result.

SUPPLICATION

Members playing in Zingaric matches are more than most earnestly requested to abstain from wearing *any* coloured shirt, jacket, or trousers. A Zingaric belt, cap, or ribbon round hat or neck, should be the only distinguishing badge.

N.B. This is a supplication and not a Regulation – and it is left to the good taste of Members to act upon it or not.

IRRITATION

'Aie!!! – There's the rub.'
Old Play

Zingaric Bowlers are requested not to become rubbers of heads, hats, caps etc., when a ball accidentally passes near a wicket. Zingaric Batsmen and Fieldsmen being hit at double or single wicket are not entitled to the rub.

PROHIBITION
Health Drinking and Dry Toasts
STRICTLY PROHIBITED

INTIMATION

If *absolutely* unable to keep the 'Promise to play', give timely notice to the head of the Eleven you disappoint.

ABNEGATION

Sacrifice self – Consider the interests of the Club – Your circle of real friends will considerably increase.

REITERATION

Keep your promise – Keep your temper – Keep your wicket up.

APPENDIX 2

Lists of Members

MEMBERS
on 31 December 1981

HRH The Duke of Edinburgh
HRH The Duchess of Kent

FREEMEN

Aird, Ronald
Allen, G. O. B.
Cassels, Field-Marshal Sir A. J. H.
Cornwallis, 2nd Lord
Crawley, C. S.
Home of the Hirsel, Lord
Kent, HRH The Duchess of
Norfolk, Lavinia, Duchess of
Ritchie, Gen. Sir N. M.

FULL-PLAY MEMBERS

Ainscough, C. H.
Aizlewood, R. P.
Allan, R. M. S.
Allerton, J. W. O.
Anderson, A. J.
Angelo Sparling, W. A.
Anton, I. A.
Ashworth, D. A.
Aspell, T. I.
Attenborough, G. M.
Awdry, V. C.
Aylen, W. S.

Bacon, N. H. P.
Bakker, C. R. P.
Baldry, D. A. J.
Barber, G. W. P.
Barber, T. D.
Barclay, J. R. T.
Barker, A. H.

Barrow, T. J.
Barton, M. D.
Baskervyle Glegg, Lt-Col. J.
Bawden, M. W.
Bebb, J. M.
Becher, J. W. M. W.
Berendt, A. P. D.
Bevan, T. J.
Birkbeck, H. C.
Black, C. A. A.
Blackham, Lt J. J., RN
Blofeld, H. C.
Bodington, P. R.
Bond, N. P.
Boone, W. R.
Bousfield, D. S.
Bovingdon, N. B.
Boyd, Hon. J. A. L.
Boyd, P. A. McN.
Braithwaite, C. E.
Brankin Frisby, J. N.
Bray, R. W. A.
Brennan, A. P. J.
Brennan, J. J. E.
Brims, C. D.
Brocklehurst, D. A.
Brodhurst, R. H. A.
Broke, S. W. S.
Brooks, P. M.
Brooks, Maj. R. M. G.
Brown, R. P.
Bruce, A. H.
Brunt, Maj. N. J. P.
Bucknall, R. J. S.
Budge, Maj. D. L.
Buik, D. B.
Burgess, S. G. F.
Burnand, Capt. G. F.
Burrows, A. R. B.
Bury, T. E. O.

Calvert Smith, David
Cameron Hayes, Capt. J. C.
Campbell, D. E. D.
Canney, P. J. C.
Capel Cure, Michael
Carless, Dr J. J.
Carlisle, K. M.
Carnegie, R. A. D.
Carroll, P. R.
Carter, C. E. P.
Cattrall, P. J.
Chamberlin, N. P. H. R.
Chamberlin, Lt-Col. P. G., RM
Charlton, J. F.
Chichester, D. S. S.
Chidgey, G. J.
Christie, R. D.
Churton, Capt. R. H.
Clayton, C. S.
Clive-Ponsonby-Fane, C. E. B.
Clover Brown, A. C.
Clover Brown, R. J.
Cobham, 10th Viscount
Coghlan, T. B. L.
Coleman, Philip
Collett, Sir I. S., Bt
Compton, R. C.
Connell, M. B.
Consett, J. P. W. P.
Cordle, A. J.
Cordle, C. H.
Cornwallis, F. W. J.
Cottenham, 8th Earl of
Coulson, B. M. L.
Courage, Lt-Col. W. J.
Craig, N. C. D.
Crawley, A. H.
Crawley, C. A. S.
Crichton Stuart, H. C.
Crocker, F. H.
Crofton, Capt. E. M.
Curtis, Maj. E. P.

Daniell, J. G. S.
Daniels, J. G. U.

Daniels, R. C.
Davis, I. E. L.
Davy, P. M.
Dawson, P. G.
de Grey, Anthony
de Grey, M. J.
Demery, E. P.
Denison Smith, Lt-Col. A. A.
Deverell, Maj. J. F.
Dewar, Capt. J. G. T.
de Zoete, N. A.
Dinwiddy, C. V.
Dinwiddy. J. R.
Dixon, M. H.
Dobbie, Lt-Col. W. I. C.
Doggart, M. W. G.
Dorman, M. S.
Douglas Pennant, Simon
Du Boulay, N. T. H.
Du Boulay, R. B. H.
Dudgeon, Dr T. A.
Duff, A. R.
Dumas, Maj. H. P. E.
Dunkels, P. R.
Dunlop, Lt-Cdr A. P. H.
Dunning, Maj. M. L.
Dunnington Jefferson, Sir M. S., Bt
Dunt, Cdr J. H.
Dunt, Cdr P. A.

Ebrington, Viscount
Eckersley, P. D. C.
Edlmann, S. R. R.
Edwards, A. W. C.
Eliot, R. F.
Ellis, Lt-Cdr J. A.
Enderby, D. J.
Evans, R. I.
Evans, Dr R. W.

Faber, M. J. J.
Faith, Lt-Col. P. W.
Farquhar, A. C.
Faulkner, Capt. M. W. B.
Fellowes, Robert
Fennell, A. T.
Fitzherbert, Hon. F. M. W.
Foot, N. R. I.
Forcey, D. J.
Fortin, R. C. G.
Foster, A. N.
Foster, D. R. J.
Freedman, R. J.
Fry, C. A.
Fuller, A. W.
Fulton, Capt. R. H. G., RM
Fursdon, E. D.
Fyfe Jamieson, D. R.

Gaisman, J. N. C.
Garnier, E. J. H.
Gay, A. C. E.
Gilliat, R. M. C.
Glennie, T. D.
Godson, M. C.
Goodeve Docker, N. E.
Goodhart, Sir R. A. G., Bt
Gore, Capt. P. W.
Gray, W. M.
Green, C. J. H.
Greenall, J. D. T.
Gretton, Cdr M. P.
Griffith, M. G.
Griffiths, P. D.
Grimston, Maj. G. C. W.
Groves, M. G. M.
Gubbins, Capt. B. E. T.
Guernsey, Lord
Guest, M. R. J.
Gwynne James, Capt. D. J.

Hamblin, C. B.
Hamilton, A. C.
Hamilton Dalrymple, J. J.
Harbottle, S. N.

Harrington Evans, A. J. C.
Hatch, P. G.
Hay, P. B.
Hazlerigg, R. H.
Herbert, Hon. H. M.
Herring, J. A.
Heywood, Lt-Col. R. J.
Heywood Lonsdale, T. N.
Hills, N. H.
Hodgkinson, J. R.
Hodgson, M. E.
Hogg, M. D. N.
Holland, C. J. T.
Holt, C. A.
Hood, H. L. A.
Hooper, J. M. M.
Hopton, C. J.
Hopton, N. C.
Horsfall, C. D.
How, D. R. O.
Howard, Capt. H. C. F., RM
Hughes, R. J. M.
Hughes Onslow, A. C.
Huskinson, T. A. L.
Hutton, R. A.

Irwin, Maj. J. J.

Jackman, Maj. B. C.
Jackson, A. G. W.
Jackson, Maj. A. J. R.
Jackson, E. J. W.
Jackson, G. L.
Jackson, R. H.
Jackson, T. R.
Jamieson, C. J. G. A.
Jay, M. H.
Jefferson, R. I.
Jeffreys, Capt. Hon. G. C. D.
Jenkins, H. R.
Johnson, R. N.
Johnston, R. B. M.
Jones, Col. J. M.
Jowett, R. L.
Joynson, G. W. H.

Kaye, Col. C. M. S.
Ker, Maj. J. S.
Keun, Maj. M. I.
Kinkead Weekes, R. C.
Knox, Lt-Col. J. S.
Knox, M. G. S.

Lane, Lt G. B. D., RN
Lane Fox, E. J.
Langdale, S. J. B.
Lea, T. M.
Lee, S. N.
Lee, W. T. S.
Leonard, J. W.
Lerwill, Maj. A. T. D.
Lewis, A. R.
Lindsay, R. E.
Lofting, J. G.
Lomer, Capt. C. R. L.
Longmore, A. N. M.
Longmore, R. M. W.
Lorimer, R.
Loudon, J. R. H.
Loveday, M. A.
Lowndes, P. G.
Lyttelton, Hon. C. C.
Lyttelton, Hon. N. M.

McCall, R. P.
McCarthy, D. R.
McCorquodale, N. E.
MacDonald, Ian
McDowall, J. I.
MacDowel, T. E.
MacFarlane, Capt. G. K.
Mackinnon, K. J.
MacLean, A. N. G.
McLean, L. R.
McLean, Capt. R. W. K.
McLeod, J. R. C.

MacLeod, R. D.
Maclure, P. S. W. K.
McMullen, F. J.
MacPherson of Pitmain, M. A. F.
Madden, C. B. de B.
Majendie, N. L.
Malcolm, A. J. E.
Mallinson, R. A.
Mann, J. J. F.
Marlow, C. R. J.
Marr, B. A. C.
Martin Jenkins, C. D. A.
Martin Smith, A. E.
Meyrick, G. C. C. T. G.
Meysey Thompson, Capt. A. M. K.
Miles, R. F. S.
Miller, R. S.
Miller, Capt. S. A. St J.
Mitchell, Capt. S. A. F.
Mogg, Lt-Col. J. N. B.
Monro, D. D. C.
Monteuuis, A. H. V.
Montgomery Massingberd, H. J.
Moorby, Capt. A. L.
Mordaunt, D. J.
Morris, C. A.
Morrison, A. S.
Moylan Jones, Cdr R. C.
Murray, I. A.
Murray Willis, J. M.

Naughten, Maj. A. P. M. J.
Nevill, Capt. C. G. R.,
Nevinson, C. J. C.
Newsom, Cdr S. J. B., RM
Nichols C. D.
Nicholson, Andrew
Nicholson, N. F.
Nickerson, William
Norris, D. W. W.
Novis, R. A.

Oakes, O. J. C.
Oldridge, D. A.
Orders, J. O. D'A.
Orders, R. W. D'A

Palmer, H. W. A.
Parker Bowles, S. H.
Parkinson, M. W.
Patrick, J. S. S.
Pawle, G. J.
Pearson, G. E. D. M.
Pearson, Rev. H. G.
Pearson, R. T.
Pease, P. R. C.
Peck, Brig. R. L.
Pelham, C. H.
Pelham, H. T.
Pelham, R. J.
Percival, R. E.
Perkins, A. C. N. A.
Perrett, D. S.
Persse, Capt. B. R. E., RM
Petherick, Capt. G. R.
Pilkington, G. W.
Pilkington, T. C.
Pockney, P. C. B.
Pocock, N. E. J.
Polk, J. R.
Pope, G. M.
Pope, Col. J. J. B.
Popplewell, N. F. M.
Powell, B. L. H.
Powell, V. A. L.
Prall, W. H.
Prest, T. W.
Prichard, M. C. T.
Priestley, R. J.
Provis, N. C.
Purser, R. H.
Pyemont, Christopher

Ramsden, T. J. P.
Raper, B. S.

Rapp, Lt J. C., RN
Rawlinson, J. L.
Rawlinson, Hon. M. V.
Reed, B. L.
Reed, T. H.
Remington Hobbs, J. P.
Remnant, Hon. P. J.
Reynolds, I. S. R.
Richardson, G. W.
Robertson, W. D.
Rogerson, M. A.
Rome, C. B. N.
Ronaldshay, Earl of
Ross, N. P. G.
Ross, W. H. M.
Ross Hurst, Maj. R. W. K.
Roundell, James
Roundell, Peter
Rowe, J. J. B.
Rowland, P. W. S.
Roxburghe, 10th Duke of
Ruck Keene, Maj. H. L.
Rudd, P. S. B.

Salisbury, Matthew
Sanders, J. R.
Saunders, C. J.
Savage, R. de Q.
Scott, D. E.
Scott, P. J. R.
Sellars, N. H. L.
Sheahan, A. P.
Sherrard, S. P.
Siddons, P. R.
Sinclair, C. J. F.
Sinclair, I. A. C.
Sinker, N. D.
Snell, C. E. M.
Soutry, T. A.
Speke, I. B.
Stanger, Capt. C. R.
Starkey, Sir J. P.
Steel, D. M. A.
Stephens, J. D.
Stevens, B. T. J.
Stevens, P. R.
Steward, M. E. K.
Stewart, A. R. E. de C.
Stoddart, D. R.
Stormonth Darling, Capt. A. J.
Stratford, N. M.
Streatfeild, M. H.
Stutchbury, Capt. P. W. F.
Style, J. R.
Summerscale, D. M.
Surridge, J. G. C.
Sutton Mattocks, C. J.
Swallow, C. J.
Swann, M. C.

Taylor, N. J. A. V.
Taylor, Sqn Ldr P. P. W.
Taylor, W. N. G.
Thorne, I. D. P.
Thorne, R. G.
Tilling, C. H.
Tindall, D. F.
Tindall, R. M.
Titchener Barrett, R. C. S.
Toft, Lt B. P., RN
Tomkin, A. R. P.
Tower, Col. A. R. S.
Townsend, J. C. D.
Townsend, J. R. A.
Travis, M. S. O.
Trentham, Lt-Cdr A. B.
Trumper, J. O.
Turner, Hon. P. N. N.

Van der Noot, Lt-Col. C. H.
Vargas, J. D. C.
Vaughan Arbuckle, Capt. D. K. T.
Venables, R. W.
Verity, T. M.
Vyvyan, Maj. C. G. C.

Wagg, A. R.
Wagg, J. J.
Wagstaffe, M. C.
Wagstaffe, Maj. P. J.
Walsh, D. R.
Watson, Maj. J. M. C.
Webber, A. H.
Webster, A. P.
Webster, R. F. C.
Webster, Maj. R. M. O.
Weedon, M. J. H.
Wells, M. E. I. A.
Westminster, 6th Duke of
White, A. A. H.
White, C. A. H.
White, C. D.
White, Capt. R. J.
White Thomson, Capt. C. T.
Wigan, Peter
Wiggin, D. P.
Wild, R. E. W.
Wilkinson, N. V. M.
Williams, C. J. W.
Williams, G. D.
Williams, J. S. W.
Williams, L. H. W.
Williams, M. V. C.
Williams, N. C.
Willis, S. L. d'A.
Wilson, G. E. N. S.
Wingfield Digby, Rev. A. R.
Wingfield Digby, J. M.
Wingfield Digby, N. J.
Wingfield Digby, S. H.
Winlaw, A. S. R. de W.
Witts, F. E. B.
Wolfe Murray, A. M.
Wood, L. G. R.
Wood, M. J. B.
Woods, P. R.
Woodwark, N. G.
Woolley, D. R.
Workman, P. J.
Worlidge, C. F.
Wright, M. F. M.
Wright, P. J. L.
Wright, R. W.
Wykes, C. J. G.
Wyndham, H. M.

Yeldham, R. J. B.
Yorke Long, R. A.

HALF-PLAY MEMBERS

Abbott, D. B.
Abell, J. N.
Abell, T. G.
Acheson Gray, C. N.
Agar, N. S.
Aird, Capt. A. S.
Aizlewood, Capt. P. G. D.
Aldenham, 5th Lord
Aldous, William
Alexander, Brig. J. D. F.
Allen, Maj. G. J.
Altham, R. J. L.
Alvingham, 2nd Lord
Anderson, P. R. H.
Annaly, 5th Lord
Anson, Maj. T. P.
Anton, J. H. H.
Archibald, Maj. D. F. M.
Arthur, Col. J. R.
Atkinson, C. R. M.

Bailey, Jack Arthur
Bailey, John Adrian
Barber, S. H.
Bardsley, J. V.
Barnes, Capt. J. D. K.

Barnes, Hon. R. A. H.
Bedford, D. W. R.
Bellamy, Capt. C. G., RM
Benda, A. C. A.
Berkeley, R. J. G.
Bevan, J. G.
Beverley, H. Y. La R.
Bewsher, Col. H. F. O.
Biggs, Maj. I. E. G.
Bishop, D. B. G.
Blackshaw, W. S.
Blake, Rev. P. D. S.
Bleackley, J. W. E.
Blofeld, J. C. C.
Blount, Sqn Ldr C. C.
Boddington, R. M. H.
Bonham Carter, Hon. M. R.
Bowman, Richard
Bramall, Gen. Sir E. N. W.
Brennan, Col. R. M.
Brocklehurst, B. G.
Bromley Davenport, W. A.
Brooke, P. L.
Brooks, R. A.
Buchan, Capt. D. W. S.
Buckingham, Prof. A. D.
Bull, O. R. S.
Burney, J. C. D. E.
Burr, R. M. J.
Burton, R. H.
Burton Brown, Michael
Bushby, M. H.
Buxton, A. E.

Calvert, Capt. M. J.
Campbell, I. P.
Campbell, Lt-Col. R. A., RM
Capel Cure, G. R.
Carless, Capt. R. P. RM
Carr, D. B.
Carr, D. N.
Carter, Lt-Col. G. R. W.
Cazalet, E. S.
Chapman, Cdr D. J. R.
Chappell, Lt-Col. R. H.
Cheshire, C. S.
Chesterton, G. H.
Chignell, Maj. M. G. P.
Chinnery, Gp Capt. H. M.
Clay, W. L. S.
Clegg, Maj. D. H.
Clive, H. A.
Cobham, M. D.
Cockell, M. H.
Coke Wallis, R. C.
Coles, W. N.
Collins, W. J.
Colthurst, G. S. O. A.
Colthurst, Sir R. La T., Bt
Conington, Maj. D. E.
Connell, D. A. M.
Coombe, Lt-Col. F. A.
Cornell, Lt-Col. J. R.
Coulman, M. R.
Coulter, J. J. S., RM
Cowdrey, M. C.
Crace, C. E.
Craig, R. V.
Crawley, E. G. C.
Crutchley, Edward
Cumming, J. G.

Dashwood, Sir F. J. V. H., Bt
Dawson, A. J. N.
Dawson, E. A.
Dawson, T. M. E.
Day, A. S.
Delisle, G. P. S.
Denne, T. G.
Dennis, C. M.
de Rothschild, E. R. A.
Deshon, Maj. D. P. T.
Dickinson, Maj. A. J.
Dilhorne, 2nd Viscount
Doggart, G. H. G.
Dowding, A. L.

Downing, J. C. R.
Dunphie, Col. C. C.
Durden Smith, Neil
Dymoke Marr, P. J. C.
Dyson, E. M.

Eckersley, P. L.
Eckersley, R. A.
Eden, Maj. J. A.
Ellwood, Col. P. J.
Evans, D. W. R.

Faber, J. G.
Fairbairn, G. B.
Faithful, J. D. T.
Falcon, Antony
Farmer, J. J. S.
Farmiloe, M. J.
Farr, B. H.
Fasken, D. K.
Fenwick, N. A.
Ferguson, Maj. R. I.
Fetherstonhaugh, C. B. R.
Findlay, Lt-Cdr J. M.
Fisher, A. N. S.
Fletcher, R. A.
Flint, E. R.
Forbes, Capt. W. F. E.
Ford, Lt-Cdr J. W.
Foster, C. F.
Foster, W. J.
Francis, G. C.

Gardiner Hill, P. F.
Gardiner Hill, R. T.
Garnett, M. N.
Gatehouse, R. A.
Gay, I. P. E.
Gibson, C. H.
Glendyne, 3rd Lord
Goold, J. S.
Gordon, Maj. J. L. H.
Gordon Lennox, Brig. B. C.
Gore, Maj. T. C.
Gracey, R. M. K.
Gray, D. A. A.
Gray, Dr K. W.
Greener, Maj. W. J. M.
Gridley, R. C.
Griffiths Lloyd, F. R.
Grove, Maj. B. P.
Guilford, D. J. S.
Gunnery, Cedric
Guthrie, A. C.
Guy, Gen. Sir R. K.

Hale, J. H.
Hambro, C. E. A.
Hardy, Col. E. M. P.
Hardy, R. H.
Hare, Sir Thomas, Bt
Havergal, Col. H. M. C.
Hawke, Dr C. R. J.
Hawkins, Capt. R. H.
Hely Hutchinson, H. A.
Henderson, Derek
Henley Welch, D. F.
Hichens, A. L.
Hill, J. R. L.
Hill Wood, Sir D. B., Bt
Hill Wood, P. D.
Hoare, Francis
Hoare, M. D.
Hobbs, J. A. D.
Hodgson, Maj. B. J.
Hopkins, Maj. J. O.
Hordern, C. N. H.
Hordern, P. M.
Hoyer Millar, G. C.
Hudson, Lt-Gen. Sir Peter
Hughes Games, Lt-Cdr G. M.
Hulbert, D. J.
Huskinson, G. M. C.

Illingworth, J. H. H.
Impey, C. A.

Impey H. E.
Ingleby Mackenzie, A. C. D.

Jackson, J. G. C.
Jameson, W. S. M.
Jarmain, Maj. D. T.
Jenkinson, J. C. L.
Jones, F. A.
Joynt, H. W.

Keeling, M. E. A.
Keighley, Hon. W. G.
Keightley, Maj.-Gen. R. C.
Kemp, D. S.
Kenny, Maj.-Gen. B. L. G.
Kidd, Rev. J. A.
Kimmins, S. E. A.

Lane, Brig. B. M.
Lardner, T. J. E.
Lawrence, W. N. M.
Leaf, J. F.
Lee, Col. C. J.
Legge, P. B.
Leigh Pemberton, Robert
Leschallas, A. G. P.
Leslie, Robin
Lewis, H. G.
Lindsay, Hon. Patrick
Liverpool, Bishop of
Lomax, I. R.
Lowe, D. B. D.
Ludlow, M. R.
Lupton, C. J.
Lyster, G. L.

McAlpine, R. J.
McCarthy, Lt-Col. R. H. G.
McCausland, Col. I. H.
McCorquodale, Alastair
McDonnell, Maj. T. R. N.
McLachlan, I. M.
McLeod, Sir Charles, Bt

Maclure, Sir J. R. S., Bt
McMullen, J. C.
Macnutt, R. P. S.
Maitland, P. J.
Mallett, C. M.
Marlar, R. G.
Marr, D. A. C.
Marshall, J. C.
Marsland, G. P.
Martineau, M. J. T.
Matheson, C. I. A.
May, P. B. H.
Mayes, Brig. C. M. A.
Maynard, Maj. Martin
Mellor, H. S.
Melluish, M. E. L.
Metaxa, P. A.
Metcalfe, S. G.
Mitchell, I. N.
Montagu Douglas Scott, Capt. D. A.
Monteagle, 6th Lord
Morse, M. H.
Morton, M. M.
Mountgarret, 17th Viscount
Myrtle, Brig. A. D.
Myrtle, G. H. J.

Napier, R. S.
Neame, A. R. B.
Neame, R. H. B.
Newman, Col. H. E. H.
Newman, Robin George
Newman, Roger Grant
Nickerson, M. O. J.

Pailthorpe, M. W.
Palmer, Sir G. C. J., Bt
Pank, Brig. J. D. G.
Parker Jervis, Maj. Roger
Parkes, Capt. M. G. H.
Parsons, A. C.
Pearson, T. M.

Pease, G. E. C.
Peel, J. C.
Peet, F. A.
Peppiatt, D. R.
Phillips, D. C. S.
Pilkington, Sir T. H. M. S., Bt
Pinney, G. H.
Popplewell, O. B.
Porchester, Lord
Prior, Maj. D. C.
Prior, Rt Hon. J. M. L.
Prodger, J. A.
Pyman, Maj. H. A. M.

Raison, J. P.
Ramus, Wg Cdr A. A.
Rankin, A. M.
Rankine, R. P.
Reid, J. R.
Reynard, P. E.
Richardson, Maj. M. J. B.
Ricketts, M. R.
Rimell, A. G. J.
Roberts, Brig. J. M. H.
Roberts, Rear Admiral J. O.
Roberts, Lt-Col. J. S.
Robertson, J. B.
Robinson, A. L. a'C.
Robson, C. H. W.
Roynon, G. D.
Rudd, C. R. D.

Sainsbury, S. D. D.
Sanderson, Lancelot
Savill, T. R. H.
Scott, Sir J. W., Bt
Seaton, Maj. G. S.
Sellar, Lt-Cdr M. D. M.
Selley, Maj. W. T.
Shakerley, Sir G. A., Bt
Shennan, Maj. M. K.
Silk, D. R. W.
Singleton, Sir E. H. S.
Skinner, T. J. M.
Smail, Maj. S. T.
Smeeth, T. J. H.
Smiley, Maj. J. P.
Smith, A. C.
Smith, C. M.
Speer, R. G. T.
Spencer, 8th Earl
Spooner, E. H.
Squire, A. H.
Stafford, 4th Lord
Stafford, Maj. H. G. H.
Stephenson, Col. J. R.
Still, Col. N. M.
Stoddart, P. L. B.
Stormonth Darling, R. A.
Street, Hon. A. A.
Stuart, R. B.
Stubbs, Rev. A. R. P.
Studd, Sir E. F., Bt
Summers, T. R.
Surridge, J. G. C.
Sweeney, J. P.
Symington, Maj. S. J.

Taplin, Lt-Col. J. A., RM
Taylor, E. J. T.
Taylor, Capt. F. J. B.
Taylor, M. E.
Thicknesse, J. D.
Thomas, Capt. Sir G. M. D., Bt
Thorne, Maj.-Gen. D. C.
Thorne, Lt-Col, M. E.
Tillard, Capt. J. R.
Tingey, Lt-Col. M. J. W.
Tower, Maj. A. R. S.
Tower, Lt-Col. P. G. S.
Toynbee, L. L. F.
Tozer, Lt.-Col. J. R.
Trasenster, Capt. D. R. de C.
Trasenster, Maj. M. A. T.
Travers, T. C.
Treherne Thomas, R. K. F. C.

Tress, M. J. C.
Trubshaw, E. B.
Twistleton Wykeham Fiennes,
Very Rev. Hon. O. W.

Umbers, R. H.
Usher, Capt. T. G.

Vickers, Maj.-Gen. R. M. H.
Vivian, Brig. A. C.

Waldock, H. E.
Walker, B. R. J.
Walton, A. C.
Ward, Maj. R. W.
Wardington, 2nd Lord
Watney, D. C.
Watts, G. E.
Webb, Dr H. E.
Weld, W. J.
Welsh, Brig. P. M.
Weston, Rear Admiral C. A. W.
Wheeler Bennett, R. C.
Whitamore, J. A.
Whitcombe, P. A.
Whittle, C. J. R.
Wilenkin, B. C. G.
Williams, Capt. A. D.
Williams, C. C. P.
Williams, Lt-Col. D. S.
Williams, E. L.
Wilson, E. R. P.
Wimperis, Dr E. J.
Winter, N. A. J.
Withall, Maj.-Gen. W. N. J.
Wolfe Murray, J. A.
Wollocombe, Maj. P. A. S.
Wollocombe, R. H.
Woodcock, Brian
Woodcock, J. C.
Woodhouse, A. J. P.
Woodhouse, G. E. S.
Worlidge, P. F.
Worsley, G. O.
Worsley, J. A.
Wrigley, M. H.
Wynne, O. R. W.

CANDIDATES FOR THE ASYLUM FOR AGED AND DECAYED ZINGARI

Aarvold, His Hon. Judge C. D.
Abell, Sir G. E. B.
Adam, Gen. Sir R. F., Bt
Agar, W. T.
Aird, Ronald
Akers Douglas, A. G.
Allen, A. W.
Allen, G. O. B.
Allom, M. J. C.
Anstruther Gough Calthorpe, Sir
R. H., Bt
Archer, Col. G. F. H.
Arrowsmith, R. L.
Aubrey Fletcher, Sir J. H. L., Bt
Awdry, A. L.
Bailey, Sir D. T. L., Bt
Barber, A. T.
Baring, A. E. G.
Barrett, Cdr D. H. B.
Barton, B. D.
Barton, M. R.
Bean, Lt-Col. J. R.
Bean, Col. L. H.
Beaufort, 10th Duke of
Becher, Sir W. F. W., Bt
Belper, 4th Lord
Benn, Antony
Bewicke, Maj. Calverly
Binny, J. A. F.
Bird, T. A.

Birkbeck, Henry
Blake, Lord
Blunden, Sir William, Bt
Borwick, Maj. P. M.
Bousfield, D. G.
Boyall, Cdr A. J.
Boys, Cdr F. C.
Brice, W. C. W.
Brocklehurst, Maj.-Gen. A. E.
Brodhurst, A. H.
Bromley Davenport, Edward
Bromley Davenport, Lt-Col. Sir W. H.
Brooke, Vice Admiral B. C. B.
Brown, F. R.
Buchanan, J. D.
Bullock Marsham, A. J.
Bullock Marsham, C. G.
Burns, Maj.-Gen. Sir W. A. G.
Burridge, J. D.
Buxton, D. G.

Caccia, Lord
Cadogan, Col. E. H.
Campbell, Maj. E. F. D.
Campbell, Sir G. T. H., Bt
VC Campbell, Brig. L. M.
Campbell, N. K. G.
Campbell, Rt Hon. Sir R. I.
Capel Cure, G. N.
Carew Pole, Sir J. G., Bt
Carlisle, K. R. M.
Carnegie, Maj. Hon. J. D.
Cassels, Field Marshal Sir A. J. H.
Caswell, E. H.
Cave, A. D.
Chenevix Trench, Maj. R. A.
Chetwode, Maj. G. D.
Clark, D. G.
Clay, G. L.
Clive, D. G.
Clover Brown, Charles
Cobbold, R. H.
Coleridge, F. J. R.
Collins, Sir A. J. R.
Collins, Maj. H. A.
Collins, Vere
Cooper Key, Lt-Col. E. A.
Cornwallis, 2nd Lord
Cornwallis, Hon. F. N. W.
Coxwell Rogers, Maj.-Gen. N. A.
Crawley, A. M.
Crawley, C. S.
Crawley, K. A. G.
Cripps, J. H.
Cunliffe, Capt. R. L. B., RN
Cunningham, Lt-Gen. Sir H. P.

Darell, Brig. Sir J. L., Bt
Darling, Lt-Gen. Sir K. T.
Darwall Smith, R. F. H.
Davies Scourfield, Col. D. G.
Davies Scourfield, Maj. John
Day, Cdr E. C. L.
Dean, P. W. M.
Deighton, Maj. J. H. G.
Delamere, 4th Lord
Dewhurst, H. L.
de Zoete, M. H.
Dixon, Dr G. E.
Dixon, G. H.
Donnelly, M. P.
Douglas Home, Hon. E. C.
Drew, Maj. John
Du Boulay, Lt-Col. M. H. H.
Dunbar, J. G.
Duncan, Col. A. A.
Dunlop, Rear Admiral C. C. H.
Dunne, Maj. N. G. F.

Ebbisham, 2nd Lord
Eggar, J. D.
Ellwood, Capt. M. O. D., RN
Enderby, Col. Samuel
England, R. M.
Evans, Capt. M. J., RN

Farebrother, M. H.
Farmiloe, M. D. B.
Ferrand, Lt-Col. S. H.
ffrench Blake, Maj. M.A.O'B.
Fisher, Hon. F. F.
FitzGerald, T. G.
Fleming, I. D. K.
Forbes, Lt-Col. W. D. H. C.
Ford, Sir E. W. S.
Ford, N. M.
Ford, Gp Capt. W. R.
Forster, F. M. M.
Foster, Maj.-Gen. N. L.
Foster, P. G.
Foster, Brig. R. H. A.
Frankland, Hon. R. N.
Franks, B. M. F.

Garnier, Maj. E. H. C.
Gascoyne, A. S. B.
Gay, Maj. A. W.
Gay, Maj. D. W. M.
Gillett, Maj. H. F. D.
Goodall, Maj. K. M.
Gore, Brig. A. C.
Gore, J. F.
Gore Browne, Sir T. A.
Gornall, Capt. J. P., RN
Gosling, R. B.
Gourlay, Gen. Sir B. I. S.
Graaf, Sir de Villiers, Bt
Grace, Lt-Col. G. F.
Grace, Col. H. R.
Grace, O. J.
Grenfell, H. St L.
Grieve, Maj. C. F.
Griffin, Maj. P. S. D.
Griffith, S. C.
Grimston, Lt-Col. G. S.
Grover, J. N.
Guise, J. L.
Guise, J. L. T.
Gurney, Brig. C. H.

Hadlee, W. A.
Haig, Lt-Col. A. E. G.
Hale, K. F. H.
Hammond, Cdr R. J. L.
Hammond Chambers Borgnis, D. C.
Hammond Chambers Borgnis, R. P.
Harbord, W. E.
Harbottle, Brig. M. N.
Harris, 5th Lord
Harris, Brig. L. J.
Hawke, 9th Lord
Hawker, Sir F. C.
Hazlerigg, 2nd Lord
Hazlerigg, Hon. T. H.
Heaven, Maj. R. J. G.
Hedley, Maj. W. K.
Henderson, Admiral Sir N. S.
Henley, Maj. R. A.
Hewan, G. E.
Hewetson, Gen. Sir R. H.
Hill, A. E. L.
Hill, B. J. W.
Hill Wood, C. K. H.
Hill Wood, D. J. C.
Hoban, B. M. S.
Hodgson, Lt-Col. C. V.
Hogg, Sir J. N.
Holderness, Lord
Holderness, Rt Rev. G. E.
Holme, Maj.-Gen. M. W.
Holmes, Lt-Col. R. N. B.
Holt, R. A. A.
Home of the Hirsel, Lord
Hornby, M. C. St J.
Horton Fawkes, Major Le G. G. W.
Hotchkin, N. S.
Howard, J. W.
Howard Dobson, Gen. Sir P. J.
Howe, 6th Earl
Howes, Rear Admiral P. N.

Hudson, Brig. R. E. H.
Hughes, Brig. P. M.
Hughes Hallett, Lt-Col. N. M.
Huskinson, G. N. B.

Imbert Terry, Maj. Sir E. H. B., Bt
Incledon Webber, Lt-Col. E. S.

Jacob, Lt-Gen. Sir E. I. C.
Jameson, Capt. T. G. C., RN
Jamieson, Rear Admiral I. W.
Johnston, B. A.
Joynson, W. R. H.

Kaye, M. A. C. P.
Keith Jones, Maj.-Gen. Richard
Kemp, M. F.
Keown Boyd, Col. W. D.
Kershaw, Peter
Kidd, E. L.
King Martin, Brig. J. D.
Kingsley, M. H.
Kingsley, Sir P. G. T.
Knight, R. J.

Lambton, Cdr Hedworth
Lane Fox, Lt-Col. F. G. W.
Lane Fox, J. H.
Lascelles, Lt-Col. R. G.
Lee, His Honour Judge A. M.
Lee, Capt. E. H., RN
Leeming, Dr J. A. L.
Legard, A. R.
Lewis, Lt-Col. A. W. D.
Lighton, Lt-Col. Sir C. R., Bt
Linlithgow, 3rd Marquess of
Linton, Col. J. E. F.
Lithgow, Brig. A. O. L.
Lithgow, Lt-Col. W. S. P.
Llewelyn Davies, Nicholas
Loudon, F. W. H.
Lowndes, W. G. L. F.
Lowry, Lt-Col. M. A.
Lubbock, C. W. S.
Lucas, Brig. H. F.
Lumby, Capt. M. G. R., RN
Lupton, W. A.
Lyon, Col. W. G.

McCall, Lt-Col. Barney
McGaw, Lt-Col. A. J. T.
McGaw, R. T.
Macindoe, D. H.
Mackenzie, Brig. K. S.
Mackessack, Lt-Col. Kenneth
Maclean, Col. J. F.
Macnab, Brig. Sir G. A. C.
Mann, F. G.
Mann, J. P.
Manners, Cdr E. A. S.
Marriott, Maj.-Gen. Sir J. C. O.
Marsham, Cdr H. A. L.
Marten, Lt-Cdr G. G.
Martin, R. C.
Martin, Cdr R. H.
Maturin Baird, Col. C. E.
Melville, Alan
Mennim, Frank
Milbank, Maj. Sir M. V., Bt.
Millett, Wg Cdr C. B.
Mills, J. M.
Mogg, Gen. Sir H. J.
Monckton, 2nd Viscount
Montagu Douglas Scott, Lt-Col. J. H.
Mordaunt, E. J.
Mordaunt, R. C.
Mott Radclyffe, Maj. Sir C. E.
Munro, R. M.
Murray Johnson, Lt A. F., RN

Nash, P. G. E.
Nevill, Maj.-Gen. C. A. R.
Nevinson, J. H.

Newman, G. C.
Noble, Rt Hon. M. A. C.
Norfolk, Lavinia, Duchess of

Oldfield, P. C.
Ormerod, Maj. Sir C. B.
Oswald, Maj.-Gen. M. St J.
Owen Smith, H. G.

Page, Lt-Col. R. K.
Palmer, C. H.
Palmer, G. E. H.
Palmer, Lt-Col. R. H.
Paris, C. G. A.
Parker, Maj. F. A. V.
Patterson, C. R.
Pawle, J. H.
Pawson, A. G.
Pawson, H. A.
Pawson, P. H. C.
Pearson, G. T.
Peddie, Maj.-Gen. Graham
Perkins, Lt-Col. Æ. J. M.
Pether, Stewart
Phayre, Brig. R. A.
Phillimore, Cdr R. A. B.
Pilkington, R. C. L.
Ponsonby, Lt-Cdr R. M. D.
Powell, A. G.
Powell, R. W.
Pragnell, M. W.
Pretyman, Sir W. F.
Pridham, Lt-Col. J. E.
Priestley, R. H.
Pulbrook, Roger

Quill, Col. R. H., RM

Radcliffe, H. J. R. J.
Randolph, R. S.
Read, H. D.
Remington Hobbs, Lt-Col. Edward

Ritchie, Gen. Sir N. M.
Roberts, Gen. Sir O. L.
Robertson, R. M.
Robson, C. G. W.
Rochdale, 2nd Viscount
Romilly, 4th Lord
Rowan, Maj. R. C.
Ruffer, A. M.
Ruggles Brise, Sir J. A., Bt
Russell, D. L.

Sale, Richard
Saye & Sele, 21st Lord
Sayer, Cdr J. D.
Scott, Lt-Col. H. E.
Sellar, Cdr K. A.
Seymour, Maj. W. N.
Shaw, Capt. R. J., RN
Shearer, E. D. R.
Sheepshanks, C. E. W.
Sherlock, Rev. G. H. K.
Sherrard, Patrick
Shortt, Maj.-Gen. A. C.
Shuckburgh, Sir C. G. S., Bt
Simpson, Col. F. W.
Simson, M. R. F.
Sinclair, 17th Lord
Sinclair, Col. T. C.
Singleton, A. P.
Singleton, Col. G. M.
Singleton, Maj. J. F. M.
Skene, R. W.
Smiley, Maj. C. M.
Southby, Lt-Col. Sir A. R. C., Bt
Southesk, 11th Earl
Standage Lt-Col. D. L. F. M.
Stanley Clarke, Brig. A. C. L.
Stanning, John
Stanton, Maj.-Gen. A. F.
Stephens, Sir David
Stephenson, Col. J. W. A.
Stoop, Lt-Cdr I. M.
Stuart French, R. F. H. P.

Studd, Sir P. M.
Surtees, Maj. J. F. H.
Sutton, M. A.
Swanton, E. W.
Sykes, Maj. H. H.

Tanner, J. D. P.
Taylor, Maj. A. R.
Tennyson, Hon. M. A.
Terry, P. N. L.
Tew, J. E.
Thackara, Cdr A. L. S. S.
Thomas, Maj.-Gen. G. A.
Thompson, J. R.
Thorne, George
Thornycroft, Col. G. M.
Tilling, T. H.
Tindall, Mark
Townsend, D. C. H.
Tremlett, Maj.-Gen. E. A. E.
Troughton, Sir C. H. W.
Tuck, Capt. G. S., RN
Tuff, Col. C. R.
Tufnell, Capt. M. N., RN
Turnbull, M. T.
Twiss, Vice Admiral Sir F. R.
Tyler, Lt-Col. A. W.

Valentine, B. H.
Van Straubenzee, Lt-Col. H. H.
Van Straubenzee, Col. P. T.
Vickers, Brig. A. W. N. L.
Villiers, Hon. W. N. S. L. H.

Waddy, Rev. L. H.
Walker, Maj. J. C.
Walker, P. A.
Walker, R. R. C.
Warner, J. J. P. F.
Weatherby, J. H.
Webster, W. H.
Weld Forester, C. R. C.
Welman, E. M. P.
Westmacott, R. V. C.
Wethered, R. H.
Whatman, J. D.
White, Capt. A. J. R., RN
White, Capt. R. T., RN
Wigan, Sir A. L., Bt
Wildish, Vice Admiral D. B. H.
Wilkinson, Col. W. A. C.
Willcocks, Maj. J. F.
Williams, Sir E. T.
Wilson, Lt-Gen. Sir A. J.
Wilson, Maj. C. J.
Wilson, D. C.
Wilson, Rev. Michael
Wilson, Col. N. J.
Winlaw, A. W. E.
Winn, Hon. R. H.
Winnington, Col. T. F. C.
Wolfe Murray, Lt-Col. M. V. A.
Wyld, J. H. G.
Wynyard, E. J. B.

Young, D. E.

ATTACHÉE

Leigh Pemberton, Mrs Robin